GRAVE SECRETS

MARY HICKS GUNN

Copyright © September 2016 by Mary Dean Hicks-Gunn

All rights reserved. No part of this publication may be reproduced, or transmitted in any form or by any mean, including photocopying, recording or other electronic or mechanical methods, without the prior written permission of the publishers, except in the case of brief quotations embodied in critical reviews and certain other noncommercial uses permitted by copyright law.

Printed in the United States of America

Cataloging-in-Publication data Hicks-Gunn, Mary Dean
Grave Secrets: Mary Dean Hicks-Gunn 208p. 6 in. × 9 in.
1. Non-Fiction 2. Drama 3. Mystery I Hicks "Grave Secrets" First Edition

Cover Illustration and Historical photographs by Mary Dean Hicks-Gunn
Editing by Mary Dean Hick-Gunn

For permission requests, write to publisher, addressed
"Attention: Permissions Coordinator" at the address below.
133 Elizabeth Lane
Sylacauga, Al 35150

Ordering Information:
Quantity sales. Special discounts are available on quantity purchases by corporations, associations, and others. For details, contact the publisher at the address above.
This book is **Based on a True Story**. As an actual accurate memoir of my life story and the life of my deceased husband. Content Advisory: Mature Audiences.

Copyright © September 2016 Mary Dean Hicks-Gunn. All rights reserved.

ISBN-13: 978-1791674427

Dedication

I want to dedicate this book to my loving daughter who has kept me from falling into a state of despair and self-hatred. She has helped me to see that self-criticism and unmet expectations are only prequels to success. My girl is a real gem.... a real Krystal.

Contents

Foreword vii
CHAPTER 1 Growing Pains 1
CHAPTER 2 The Leap 16
CHAPTER 3 Prom Night 23
CHAPTER 4 Hear No Evil 29
CHAPTER 5 See No Evil 34
CHAPTER 6 Do No Evil 38
CHAPTER 7 Motherless Child 51
CHAPTER 8 Hicks 55
CHAPTER 9 Till Death Do Us Part 113
CHAPTER 10 Tattletales 143
CHAPTER 11 Brown Eyed Girl 166
CHAPTER 12 Karma 173
CHAPTER 13 Seeking Closure 181
Photographs & Documents 193

Foreword

This book will set me free. Free from a life of what if's, why not's, and may I's. I've been sitting on a stack of memories for what seems like forever and now my heart and mind are ready for a release. These memories were painfully locked away inside me for 40 plus long years along with the pressure of containing them, and maintaining them. It has had a real impact on my life, but now it's time to let go and let the true healing begin.

This is an unsolved true story about my husband. His name was James Edward Hicks. His friends and family called him "Hicks." Hicks was a young man who was full of life but had a very short one because he was cut down in his prime. We were together for four short years, and were married for two of those years. From this union God blessed us with one child; a daughter. Hicks adored her, but would only get to be in her life for 2 ½ years. When I look back, remembering Hicks face as he lay in his casket. I still wonder what his last thoughts were before his life was taken from him. From his swollen eyes, and half open hands that almost made fists, I could tell he didn't go without a fight. I also think about how hurtful it must have been to have had someone that you trusted and loved to reveal their true identity to you, while your life was ending.

1.

GROWING PAINS

I WAS A SHY COUNTRY GIRL, the oldest of eight children; four boys and four girls. I was raised in a three-room shack with my parents along with my siblings. My dad was a pulpwood truck driver, weekend drunk, and womanizer. He was what you call a "rolling stone." Although my dad was a hard worker, we couldn't tell because he never brought any of his earnings home to us. I loved my dad with all my heart; all of us did. He never reciprocated that love because he was too busy hurting my mom and chasing other women to even care. To this day, I can't recall my dad ever hugging me or any of my siblings, and so the early part of my life was filled with feelings of being unloved, and it caused me to be very withdrawn.

My mother was a stay at home mom, who seemed to always be sad and angry. It was mainly because she was mistreated and neglected by my dad. She was a good wife and mom, who tried to do her very best for us. Since she also depended on my dad's income, that he rarely provided, I often watched as she sat many nights at our small dinner table refusing to eat because it was only enough for me and my siblings. I would watch as she scraped our plates after we finished eating, hoping for remnants, and sometimes there weren't any. I often think that if my mom had gotten an education, things would have been better for her and her children. She was only 15 years old when she got pregnant with me. She was too young to take care of herself, let alone a bunch of babies. My dad was seven years older than my mom, so he had an advantage over her mentally and physically. I constantly witnessed the abuse he inflicted upon her. The violence played a vital role in my childhood which was full of fear and stress; especially when my dad threatened to line each of us up and "Kill everything that was big enough to sop syrup." My dad's failure to provide left us poor and hungry; creating continual conflict between he and my mother. But, no matter how much they were at each other's throat, you could rest assured that every nine months there would be another mouth to feed. Not only another mouth, but another person that I would be responsible for taking care of.

My mom tried to make my dad happy, but he would constantly start brutal fights to get out of the house, so he could be with his other women. My mom not only endured his violence, but the public shame and humiliation from the women in the area from whom my dad committed adultery with. My mother finally became overwhelmed and fed up, but instead of packing us up and leaving him, she packed up and left us with him; taking our youngest infant sibling with her. This further created an even more terrible situation for my siblings and me. Now, we were motherless and lost, and with a dad who also didn't want to be responsible and tied down with us. It wasn't long before he got rid of us too, so I guess you could say that we became motherless and fatherless.

The day after my mom left, my dad took us to my mom's distant relatives house and left us there. My mom's relatives were just as poor as we were, if not more, and even had more children. My dad just dropped us off and left. He didn't leave any money, bring any food, nor did he even make sure that we had a clean change of clothes. When he left us there, we were there for weeks, and those weeks seemed like forever.

Now let me tell you about my mom's relative's house. It was a shack as well and reeked of piss and other foul odors. There was only one chair and one bed. Moments after we arrived and my dad left, I remember being placed on that bed, and my pants were removed. I was then examined by the man of the house and his son while the wife looked on. I believe I was four going on five at the time. Although I was young, I remember feeling very embarrassed and ashamed. I don't remember being touched in any way, and quite possibly he may have checked me to make sure that I wasn't in diapers. I don't know, but I just remember feeling very uncomfortable lying there being searched with their eyes. Each night, we slept on the floor in a corner of the small house. I remember a lot of stomach pains because I was so hungry. My two siblings were hungry too. I remember their cries to me asking, "When is momma and daddy coming back?" I remember telling them, "Don't cry, they'll be back."

The days there lingered on, and finally one-day, daddy came back to see us. We were so happy because we thought that he was coming to rescue us from that hell hole that we had been confined to. Unfortunately, it was just to visit, and it was going to be a short one because he was there only for a minute before he tried to leave. When he was about to leave, we began to cry and scream. We literally begged him to take us with him. He told us that he couldn't and said that it was because he had to go to work, and there wasn't anyone to watch us. I remember pleading with him and telling him how I could take care of us, if he would only let me. He ignored my pleas and continued to walk towards his car. As he opened the door to get in, my younger sister caught his eyes as he peered across the yard at her pulling tree bark from a big rotting oak tree and eating it. This visual showed our dad that we were not only very hungry, but we were no better off with the relatives. I guess that this was the reality check he needed to get us the hell out of there before we literally starved and died. He told us all to get in the car, then told us that he was going to take us to our Big Momma's house; our paternal grandmother.

I'll never forget that emotional trip to Big Momma's house that day. It was filled with unspoken words, a lot of tears, and gladness that we were leaving the relative's home. When we arrived, our daddy dropped us off and kept going on his merrily way, and I don't even think he gave us a second glance before he took off. Our Big Momma's house was vacant because she only used the house during summertime. Her actual home was in Mobile, Alabama. The doors to the house were not locked, so we just pushed our way on in. The house was filled with natural light, but she had several kerosene lamps, and boxes of matches to light them with sitting everywhere. Most of all, she had food. Lots and lots of food! There was food on shelves and in pantries. She even had a few chickens in a coop outside that laid eggs. The chickens were being taken care of by my daddy's brother, who lived up the road with their grandmother. My daddy was not close to his brother nor his grandmother, so he threatened us as we arrived that if we went to visit them, he would take us back to the relative's house. Of course, we obeyed because we didn't want to go back.

I believe I was four and a half years old at the time; when the big responsibility of caring for my siblings was given to me. I remember picking up sticks to make fires in the fireplace, and cooking bread and eggs over open coals. Every time the chicken would lay an egg, my brother would go and get it. Usually, it was only one egg; but with the eggs, bread, and Big Momma's supply of sorghum syrup, we would have a meal. That would be our breakfast, lunch, and dinner because that was all that I knew how to prepare. We were three young children left alone to fend for ourselves, with no mom or dad that seemed to care.

Days turned in to nights, and nights into days. I continued to be big sister and mom. After some time, my momma returned. However, it was only for a short time because my daddy soon went back to his old ways. This time when my momma left, she also left the baby that was now a toddler. Now, instead of having to fend for myself and two people, I would have to fend for myself and three. It was too much for a young girl, but no one cared how I felt. I had two selfish parents that were trying to out hurt each other, but they were only hurting me, by running from their responsibilities. After some time, it seemed as if they had completely forgotten about us, and we didn't know if they were dead or alive. They were both gone for so long that we decided that we were going to go find them. One morning, we got dressed in the rags that we had, and all jumped into a broken-down car that was parked in the front yard. Our intentions were to start the car and go find them, and we had come up with the plan the night before.

The car was an older model car and had a choke on it with a push button to start it. The car was in the front yard facing a big cedar tree near and embankment and cliff. My younger brother was going to be the driver but couldn't even see over the steering wheel. My little sister sat up front with him while I sat in the back with my youngest brother. My brother would press the choke button which would make the car leap forward with each push. This just goes to show what happens when children are left alone and go without supervision for too long. We could've been killed if that car had sprung to life because only a small tree separated us from an embankment that led to the cliff. For a-long-time, my brother made attempts to start the car, but after a while we all realized that it wasn't going to start. We sat in the car and cried and talked about how we wished our mom and dad would come back home. We dried our tears and said that we weren't going to give up on trying, and we also talked about how we were going to try to start the car again.

It was starting to get late into the evening, so we had finally given up, and decided that it was time to go back into the house. But, as we were attempting to leave the broken car, a big brown shaggy dog appeared from nowhere. The dog ran past the car and went up on to our porch and lay there. We could see from the dirty windshield of the old broken car, that the dog was no normal dog. It had white foam coming from its mouth, and its eyes were red and caked with matter. It remained on the porch watching us, as we stared in fear. My brother honked the horn trying to scare the dog away, but the dog didn't move. He laid on the horn, and eventually it caused the battery to drain, and so we sat quietly staring at the dog. We stayed in the car for what seemed like hours, as our stomachs growled, and bladders swelled. Soon the sun started to set, and the dark orange sky was upon us. I thought he would never leave, but suddenly the dog leaped to its feet and came down from the porch. It stood there staring into the distance, as if it was waiting for something or someone to call its name. The dog refocused his attention back in our direction and headed straight towards the car. We sat frozen, but to our surprise and relief, it ran straight passed us. It crossed the yard and ran over in to the kudzu patch, and it disappeared off into the woods. We didn't waste a second, but quickly jumped out the car and ran into the house. Thinking back, I always believed that the dog was sent from God; not only to help take our minds off our parents, but also to teach us that the car wasn't a safe place to be, and bad things could happen if we were in it. The dog's presence was a lesson, and from that day on, we never got back in to that car again. We were even afraid to walk to the chicken coop, or to the spring to get water, but would carry a big stick with us every time we had to go.

After some time, I guess our dad started feeling guilty because he started checking on us, but the visits were always short. Maybe he was coming just to see if we were still alive. Once he saw that we were, he immediately left. Our mom wasn't checking in at all and had stayed gone for so long that I felt as if I no longer needed her. I had a routine, and it was keeping me and my siblings alive. They listened, and I was their little momma. I had adapted to my new role, until one day to my surprised, our momma came home. When she arrived, I remember running and hiding from her in a closet. I remember crouching down in that closet bitterly wishing that she would go back to where she came from. I was now the mother of the children she had abandoned, and I had so much anger and hate for her. When she drove up in the yard, I watched from the window and took off in to my hiding spot. When she entered the house, I remember her calling out my name, but I stayed hidden. After several calls, I finally came out, but so did my bitter, hot, and salty tears. I felt so neglected and betrayed by her. Now looking back, it is hard to believe that I made it out of my childhood alive. There are so many other painful memories that I still deal with from my post traumatic stressful childhood, but they'll all be revealed to you in a "Moment in Time."

Fast forwarding five years into my childhood, not much had changed. I was still a poor naïve country girl, but now living in a house filled with three additional siblings, and my still unhappy battling parents. My only desire at the time was finding a quiet place where I could focus, sing, dance, and be alone. This desire was always met by screaming babies and demanding parents who thought their children belonged to me. I was everyone's personal slave. I longed to be away from my entire family, and I remember plotting to run away. I prayed to God daily and asked Him to let me live to see thirty years old. At the time, I really didn't believe I would make it. You wouldn't believe the stress and pressure I was under as the oldest sibling of six kids. It nearly killed me, and in the process, it took all joy out of my life. I dreamt of running away and then becoming someone else. My dream was to go to Hollywood and become an entertainer. I was talented at singing and dancing, and I could have acted too if given an opportunity. However, those dreams were eventually crushed by my mom's constant pessimism and derogatory statements. She'd tell me that I wouldn't amount to much more than a someone who'd clean white people's homes. She would say, "You better learn how to clean good, cause white people aint gonna let you clean for them if you don't." It was never in my thoughts or plans to clean any white person's home, and I couldn't understand why this job was what my mother saw in my future. Now thinking back, it was the thought pattern of an uneducated woman, and at the time, that was all she could see for herself.

The other woman in my life was my overly religious paternal grandmother, who constantly warned me that God wanted me to keep myself unspotted from the world. With my naivety and poor understanding, I thought her words meant that I should keep myself hidden from the world. Like my mom, her words also hurt me mentally, and caused me to give up on my dreams, and I became even more shy and withdrawn. I literally became a recluse because I had no one to encourage me or help me gain esteem. Plus, I felt stuck because I now had six children that were placed upon me that I didn't give birth to.

Yes, home life was terrible, and I could go on and on about how terrible it was, but what was even worse was school life. At school, I was constantly picked on and teased by my peers. My teachers were abusive and treated me horribly too. Mainly, because they saw that I was dirt poor and came to school in raggedy clothes and shoes. My dad's reputation throughout the small community didn't help matters either, and further impacted my mistreatment. In addition to being horribly teased, I was often tired and hungry. Most kids go home, complete homework, do small chores, and then relax, but not me. When I got home, I had to wash dirty diapers and hang them out to dry, clean the house, and cook while my sickly and often pregnant mom dictated from her bed. Instead of sleeping, my nights were spent tending to crying babies. When the sun rose, I was responsible for getting my siblings ready for school and starting my miserable day all over again. Even though my mornings started lousy at home, I dreaded getting on the school bus the most. I knew there would be mean things said to me and my siblings all the way to school. I knew that I had to be strong for my younger siblings, so I wouldn't let them see me cry, or even admit that what was being said about us hurt me. My strength taught them how to be strong and ignore people who tried to hurt them.

After a tortuous ride on the bus, I would again have to face hateful words and sneers from my teachers once I got to school.

Most of the time, I was too tired and hungry to even care. I couldn't blame my mom because she would try to make sure we ate breakfast before we left home, but there was never a lunch time for me and my siblings because my dad never made sure that we had money. Unlike today, there was no free or reduced lunch; either you had money, or you didn't, and if you didn't you couldn't eat. With no money to eat, I experienced daily acute stomach aches and headaches, but most of all embarrassment. I had to sit and watch my classmates eat while my stomach howled. My empty stomach hindered not only my happiness but also my learning. I was often too hungry to even focus on school. I could've understood it more if my dad had been unemployed, but he worked every day and squandered his money on women and alcohol. Some of my classmates would even report things they'd heard their parents saying about my dad, and I would further shrink in embarrassment. The most hurtful thing was when one day, one of my classmates showed me money she said my dad had given to her. I guess this was hush money since my dad was at her house visiting her mom. When she told me, I believe that was the first time something said about my dad angered me. However, my anger quickly subsided with a cookie that she purchased for me. I somehow convinced her that since the money was given to her by my dad, she had to share it with me. To my surprise, she shared the money, and I was so thankful.

The next day, I got an even bigger surprise when my sixteen-year-old uncle; my dad's baby brother, returned from Mobile. I was walking down the hallway when I ran into him. When he saw me, he grabbed me up into his arms, hugged, and then kissed me. My uncle was a tall dark handsome young man and was very popular. He loved me like I was his little girl instead of his niece. I was so glad to see him. He asked where I was going, and if I was on my way to the lunch room to eat lunch. I told him that I was hungry and would like to eat, but I couldn't because I didn't have any money. My young uncle didn't hesitate. After he heard my statement, he immediately reached into his pocket and pulled out a two-dollar bill and gave it to me. He told me to go eat, gave me one last hug, and then headed in the opposite direction towards his class. The money was like Christmas, and I took off towards the lunch room. Back in those days, two dollars was like having twenty dollars because even a penny was valuable. I ate well that day, and a few days afterwards. When I got home, I hid my money and didn't let my mom know I had it because I knew I'd have to give it to her. The money was a secret that I kept to myself, and for the first time, I didn't have to share.

My uncle's return to school became a real God send. He not only made sure that I ate every day, he protected me from bullies on the bus. Many of the bullies didn't even know that we were related until one day they started in on me and my siblings, and he got up from his seat and told everyone off. He asked the girls who teased us, how could they have a crush on him when they treated his nieces and nephews so badly. I saw them searching their minds for an explanation, but again they never realized that he was our uncle. Before he took his seat, he made a decree that no-one was to say another word about us, or they'd have to deal with him. After my uncle's threat, bus rides to school became enjoyable. No one said a word when we got on the bus or off. My uncle was there watching over us, and we could now ride to school in peace.

The peace and my uncle's presence would be short lived because a couple of years later, my young wonderful uncle's life would end. I will never forget the day we got the news. I was on the porch with my aunt; his baby sister, and his mother my grandmother; who I was watching sew a dress for me by hand. Suddenly, a car came barreling down the road in a cloud of dust, and out jumped a neighbor who wanted to speak with my grandmother alone. They both went in the house, and a few moments later I heard my grandmother scream out in a chilling voice, "Oh my God, Lord have mercy!" Then I watched as my grandmother and the neighbor dashed from the house and got into the car. My young aunt ran from the porch and jumped in the car too, as I sat dumbfounded in a rocker on the porch. I yelled from the porch, "What happened?" My grandmother yelled back as the car took off, "Your uncle is dead!" The car sped up the road while dust swirled behind it. I was shocked by the statement. I remained on the porch and began talking to God. I remember begging God to please send my uncle home and let everything be a misunderstanding or a big mistake. I started crying, and through my tears and glossed over eyes, I felt a nice breeze and saw leaves that began to swirl in the yard. The leaves began to combine with dust and straw. It formed into a miniature funnel right before my eyes. The funnel began to grow taller and taller, and before I knew it, it was taller than me. It was a tall thin funnel and reminded me of my uncle's stature. It was a dust devil, and it swirled before me as if it was speaking to me through the rustling and bustling leaves and straw. I continue to watch it as it started to move to the edge of the yard. Once it reached the yard's edge, it swirled in place for a moment as if it was watching me too. Suddenly, the debris lifted off the ground and appeared to leap across the road, and then it vanished into a kudzu patch. After the funnel vanished, the silence and stillness seemed deafening. I knew in that very moment that it was my uncle's spirit coming to say goodbye to me. I felt his presence within, and I felt his absence after it disappeared. I still could not wrap my mind around the fact that he was gone, and I still did not know how he died. I sat there for as long as I could. I felt so alone. I don't think I've ever felt the loneliness that I felt that day. I rose from my grandma's rocking chair and began to run home. When I got there, my mom and other family members had gathered under a big oak tree in our front yard, and they were all sobbing. When I saw this, that is when I accepted the fact that my uncle was really gone.

My uncle lost his life while swimming in a pond with his friends. His friends said that they watched as he jumped in, and he appeared to be swimming before disappearing under the water. They said that they were not strong swimmers like him, so they couldn't aid him but went for help when he didn't resurface. His lifeless body was recovered later that afternoon. The day of my uncle's funeral was a blur to me. It was my first funeral, and I had cried until I couldn't cry anymore. I remember seeing my uncle in his casket, and he looked as if he was sleeping. I also remember having a deep desire not to be there, but I guess I wasn't ready to face the fact that I wouldn't see him anymore after that day. When it was time to bury him, he was buried in an area not far from our family house. In fact, his grave was so close to our house, that my siblings and I made a tree near his grave our play spot. He continued to remain a part of our daily lives; at least mine. I would visit his grave and talk to him as if he was still alive; telling him all that was going on with me and the world since his death. Even though my uncle was dead, I still considered him my best friend, and had a hard time letting him go. I think my constant presence at my uncle's grave concerned my dad because he soon told me to stop going there so often. I'd still go anyway and continued until we moved away a year later. Now thinking back, it saddens me to realize that during that time in my childhood, I had more in common with a dead teenager in his grave, than any living person.

After leaving the house near my uncle's grave, we move to a house and situation even poorer. We were now living closer to my mom's side of the family. She had six sisters and three brothers. Her youngest brother happened to be the same age as my uncle that I had just lost. My mom's youngest brother was a quiet respectful young man, who was completely different from his loud obnoxious siblings; including my mom. He introduced me to the joys of reading, and we connected through books. When I would visit my mom's side of the family, I would always remain in the car and read so I wouldn't have to interact with them. No matter how hot the car became during the summer, I'd remain in it while my other young cousins tried to get me out of it to play. I'd refuse, and then listen to derogatory statements by my aunts who'd say, I thought I was better than their kids. I would periodically look up from the book's pages to gaze upon hateful eyes staring maliciously at me. I'd quickly place my focus back to the pages, and act as if I didn't hear them making comments about me. My mom's younger brother would come to the car and ask if he could sit in the car with me and read. There, we'd be in the boiling hot sun flipping through pages and talking about what we had read. He soon became the replacement uncle for the one that I'd lost. I loved talking to him and being around him. I almost became as attached to him as I had my other young uncle. My heart was beginning to repair itself from the hurt I had endured, but it wouldn't be long before death would come knocking again; and tear the scabs from my healing wounds. This time, it would come for my mom's baby brother.

At the tender age of nineteen, my mom's baby brother lost his life due to mistaken identity. Since my young uncle didn't smoke or drink, he was often the designated driver for his siblings when they drank and partied. One night, he went to pick up his big brother who was very rowdy and always in to everything wrong. As my young uncle waited in the car for him, he heard a commotion coming from the house his brother was in, so he got out to investigate. As my young uncle headed in the direction of the noise and neared the front porch; the screen door swung open, and his brother bolted out of it running towards him. Immediately, a shot rang out from behind the open screen, and the bullet meant for his fleeing brother struck my young uncle in the head. It killed him instantly. My young uncle never even knew what hit him. It was another painful blow for my family, and another devastating blow for me. In less than two years, I had lost two uncles; another friend. I was only ten years old at the time of my second uncle's death. This was too much pain for a little kid to bare in such a short amount of time, but I guess God was preparing me for what was to come. What I went through as a young girl would have destroyed any young child, but it would just be the beginning of my pain, and my pain filled life.

2.

THE LEAP

THE YEARS SLOWLY CAME AND WENT, and I endured them like a zombie going through the motions. It was school then home, and then home then school. I was living and breathing, but I was dead inside. I didn't feel as if I had a real purpose to be alive, but I was too afraid to end my life; even though I constantly thought about it. I sometimes wonder if my late husband's early childhood was anything like mine because it was full of fear, stress, uncertainty, and pain.

    I still think about my husband often. One day, while thinking about him, I uncovered a forgotten childhood memory. It was a memory of our first official meeting which had taken place in first grade. My teacher had instructed me not to lean back in my chair, but I did it anyway and ended up flipping over. Due to my disobedience, my teacher made me remain on the floor as punishment. My fellow classmates laughed at me as I lay backwards on the cold hard floor with my feet in the air. I wasn't on the floor long before I was joined by a little boy, who had also flipped over his chair. When the little boy landed beside me, he was also instructed to remain there. That little boy was Hicks, and after several minutes of being on the floor, our teacher put us in the coat room together as further punishment. Once we were in the room, Hicks tried to talk to me, but I was too scared, shy, and embarrassed to speak to him. Coincidence maybe, but now I find myself thinking that Hicks and I may have been destined to be together ever since our first encounter.

The years and the school house rocked on, and soon it was nearing the end of my twelfth-grade year. I had just turned eighteen, and my life still seemed to have no purpose. But, an invite to my senior prom would later change my simple existence, and my life forever. It was March, in the year of seventy-one, and the girls in my class were excited and constantly discussing who they were going to take to the prom. I had grown tired of listening to the chatter. The prom was months away, but they were discussing who was taking whom, what was going to be worn, and what hairstyles they were going to wear. I guess I was a little jealous because I just knew I wasn't going to be able to go. After everyone made their "who are you going with" rounds; eventually I was asked. I told my classmates that I wasn't going because I didn't have anyone to go with. That wasn't my only reason. I knew financially, my family couldn't afford a dress for me, but they didn't need to know that. One of my friends heard my response and said, "Why don't you go with Hicks?" I said, "Hicks, who is that?" My friend looked at me as if I were crazy, and she was in disbelief that I didn't know him. According to her, he was on the basketball team and was very popular. I would never have known because I went straight home every day after school, and I was never allowed to attend any after school events. I later found out another reason why I didn't know Hicks, and it was because he wasn't in my senior class like he was supposed to be. He had fallen ill in first grade and missed a lot of days of school, so he was held back. At the time, I didn't remember him at all, and didn't believe that I had ever seen him before, but hoped he wasn't ugly. My friend went on to say that Hicks had told everyone that he liked me, and that he wanted to go to the prom with me. He told them however, that since it was my prom, I would have to ask him to go, but he wanted them to put the word out. I didn't believe her and resisted, as she grabbed my arm and pulled me down the hallway to go meet him.

We found Hicks standing in a doorway of a classroom. He was very handsome. He was tall with light brown eyes, light skin, and very full lips. He had a head full of thick sandy brown hair, and he wore it in a large afro. My friend called his name and he turned and faced us. When he saw me standing with her, he gave me the biggest smile. I stood there staring at him and couldn't believe I hadn't noticed that handsome guy before, but how could I when my head was always down. It was even harder to believe he had noticed me. I took a deep breath, grabbed my cup of courage, and shyly walked over to Hicks and asked him if he would like to go to the prom with me. With a big smile he quickly answered, "Yes!" My friend sneaked away and left us, and there we stood in the hallway talking. He was so laid back and easy to talk to, and my shyness melted away when I saw how down to earth and nice he was. The school bell interrupted and ended our wonderful conversation. We had to head to our next class, so I told him that I would talk to him later. When I was about to walk away, he asked me where I lived, and I blurted out my home's location without a second thought.

The very next day after school, Hicks showed up at my house. I was in the house doing my normal slave routine for my parents and siblings, when I heard one of my siblings yelled, "Here comes a truck, and it's turning in here!" My mom said, "Who in the world is that?" I was cleaning, and I peered out of the window to see Hicks getting out of the truck. I had a miniature heart attack watching him slowly walk towards my house, as my siblings sprouted from everywhere looking intently at him. He walked up to the porch where my mother was sitting, and he asked if I was home. My mother called my name, and I almost fainted; I wasn't expecting company, and I knew I had on my slave gear. I stuck my head out the door, told him I would be out in a minute, and to come on up on the porch and have a seat. I was glad to see him, but I was embarrassed at the same time because I still lived in a shack, and he would now see the conditions that my family and I were living in. Also, I was scared because my mom was suspicious when it came to boys and girls interacting, and it was because she had been a young parent herself. As I got dressed, I could hear my siblings asking him a million questions, so I hurried up and changed and went out on the porch to join them.

Once out there, I officially introduced him to my mom and siblings, and asked her if we could go for a walk. She agreed and we left the porch heading down to the creek with my siblings tagging along behind us. As we walked, he took my hand and held it. As we talked, he told me that he was looking forward to my prom night. I told him that I was too, and quickly changed the subject to how surprised I was to see him, but then told him that I was glad he came. He told me that he was too anxious to wait for school the next day, so he borrowed his cousin's husband's truck and decided to come by. He changed the subject back to the prom, and then told me how glad he was when I finally asked him. He said that he'd told several people that he liked me, and he was glad that it had finally gotten back to me.

I made our walk a short one due to the suspicious mom waiting on the porch. After only a thirty-minute walk, I suggested we turn around and head back to my house. When we got back to the house, he came completely on to the porch and said his goodbyes to me and my family. Hicks then walked back to his cousin's husband's truck and left. For the rest of the day and all night, all I thought about was Hicks. I had never felt what I was feeling. Hicks had brought me to life, and I tingled everywhere. I was like numb body parts coming back to life once blood flow resumed.

The next day, I was looking forward to going to school so I could see Hicks. When I got to school, he was standing in his classroom door waiting for me to come down the hall. When I got to him, he came over to me and put his arm around my shoulders. I shyly put my arm around his waist, and we walked down the hall together. Everyone that saw us, stared and smiled at us. We even got applauses from some of our classmates. We were a beautiful couple, and we turned heads. It was a couple of months before the prom, and our time was spent talking and getting to know each other. He told me he wanted me to meet his family, and I told him that he would soon have to meet my daddy, and I wasn't looking forward to it either. One Saturday, Hicks came to see me. We were sitting and talking on the porch when my daddy drove up. I said, "Here comes my daddy!" I was so scared and nervous because I knew my dad was going to embarrass me by saying something off the wall. Hicks and I watched as my dad approached the porch and began to climb the steps. My daddy was looking directly at me as my heart fluttered. When he got to the both of us, he looked over at Hicks and said, "Nigga, what you doin' here?" Hicks dropped his head and didn't answer, and my dad went on in the house as if he never saw Hicks or said a word. Most young men would've gotten scared and wanted to leave, but not Hicks. Once my dad entered the house, Hicks lifted his head and resumed talking as if he'd never saw my dad, and he seemed unphased by my dad's tone and words. Hicks acted like my dad didn't exist, and his bravery made me like him even more.

About a week later, Hicks came by my house to pick me up so I could go meet his family. Being young and shy, I was afraid to meet them. He assured me there was nothing to worry about because his family was nice, and I would really like them. Once we arrived, Hicks came around to my door and opened it. I got out, and he escorted me up to the front door. When I walked in, Hicks home was nice and clean, and very beautiful; nothing like the shack I lived in. As I stood there in the entrance, Hicks called out to his mom to come and meet me. Not only did she come, but several uncles, siblings, and his grandmother came into the living room. To me, it seemed like people were coming from everywhere; especially since I was only expecting to meet his mother. He introduced me as his girlfriend, and everyone said hello in unison. Then he introduced me to each of them individually. They all complimented me on being pretty, while Hicks uncles gave winks and smiled at him. They asked me to have a seat, but Hicks quickly told them we had somewhere else to go. However, it was only right back to my house. My mom had warned Hicks before we left that I was to come right back after I met his mother. He did exactly as my mom instructed. Once we arrived back at my house, I immediately said good bye to him. I needed time and space to catch my breath because I had just survived meeting his family, and that was a very big feat for a very shy person. When I enter the house, I told my mom about Hicks's beautiful home, and all the nice people I had met in his family. She seemed uninterested and distracted, so I went on to my room.

That night, I had trouble sleeping due to sheer excitement. I replayed repeatedly in my head how I wanted my prom night to go. I knew I'd first have to have something to wear, and I feared that I wouldn't. The next day, I called my young aunt who was then living in Philadelphia. I told her that I had met a guy and wanted to go to the prom but had nothing to wear. She was excited for me and promised that I didn't have to worry because she would send my prom dress. I was still uneasy, but she reassured me that she was going to take care of everything. I reluctantly became excited and thought about how I could hardly wait to go out with the young man of my dreams.

The days crawled by, but I prayed that my dress would make it on time. To my surprise, it arrived that following Friday. My dad knew that I was waiting on it, so he drove me to the local post office to pick it up. It came in a large brown box. I could hardly wait to get it home to check the contents. Although I was excited and happy, I was a little afraid my dress wouldn't fit. However, I knew a seamstress who could alter it for me if there was a problem. The seamstress was my neighbor who I often baby sat for, but that time of year was one of her busiest, so I wasn't sure if she'd have the time. Plus, she was always busy doing other things. When I got home, I opened my neatly packed package. After I removed my dress, I saw that my aunt had also included: shoes, jewelry, and hair accessories. I quickly removed my clothes and tried on the dress. The dress fit me perfectly!

3.

PROM NIGHT

PROM NIGHT FINALLY ARRIVED, and because of the gifts from my dad's baby sister, I felt like Cinderella. My dress was a long empire waist dress; yellow in color with a yellow sash. My shoes were white Mary Janes. My jewelry was gold and white, and it was a complete set containing earrings with a necklace and bracelet. My hairpiece was beautiful, and so was my white clutch purse that completed my outfit.

Hicks arrived at my house around 7:00 p.m. My siblings watched from the window as he got out of his car and approached the house, and yelled out to me, "He's here!" My dad opened the door and let him in, as I hurried to finish getting ready. I took one last glance into the mirror and proceeded out of the bedroom. All eyes were on me as I entered the room where my family waited. I watched as Hicks stood with his mouth open, and his eyes bugged looking at me. My siblings gasped when I walked in, and for the very first time in my life I felt beautiful. Hicks was quite handsome too. He had on a blue tuxedo that fit him to a tee. He held in his hand a yellow and white corsage, and once I stood in front of him, he pinned it on me. I glanced back at my parents and saw the pride in their eyes. This was also their approval of Hicks and me. It was almost time to leave, but not before my mom laid down the ground rules for our night. She instructed Hicks to have me home by eleven with no exceptions or excuses. He said, "Yes mam," and walked over and opened the front door for me; watching as I exited on to the porch. I saw him look back at my parents as he was about to close the door, and he gave them a nervous wave. I know my dad was giving him a death stare because Hicks looked at me with his eyebrows lifted in fear as he was closing the front door. Hicks then led me to the porch steps, helped me down them, and escorted me to the car. He opened my door and made sure that my dress was inside the car before he shut it, and then he trotted to his door. He was a perfect gentleman.

On our way, I asked him if he could stop and pick up one of my classmates who didn't have a date, and he agreed. When we arrived at her house, she was ready and waiting. Hicks got out of the car and escorted her down the steps. She had polio, so he was patient with her as he assisted her inside the car. Once my classmate was securely in, we headed to the prom. The prom was being held in our school's gym, and I knew it was going to be decorated beautifully. I could hardly wait to get there. I wanted to see what everyone was wearing, and I wanted them to also see me. That night, I was what the young people call, "Feeling myself."

Hicks had the radio blaring, and we were all singing along to the tunes. Even though the music was loud, we talked over it. Hicks was telling jokes, and we were laughing at them. We were in a nice car and were in cruise mode; heading down the dark road illuminated by the car's headlights. We were almost fifteen minutes into our drive when the music stopped, and the car cut off. We were driving fast, so it took some time before the car coasted to a complete stop. But when it did, so did our laughter.

We sat staring in total confusion and darkness. The dash board panel wasn't even lit. Hicks made several attempts to start the car, but the engine refused. The three of us were now stranded, and it was on one of the darkest roads in our small town; right down the road from a graveyard.

As we sat there, I started questioning Hicks about the car because I had never seen it before. He always visited me in a truck that he said belonged to his cousin's husband. Hicks responded and said, that his cousin's husband's truck was being worked on, so he borrowed his uncle's wife's car. I said okay, and then asked if he remembered to put gas in it, and he said he had. I then said, "Maybe your aunt had mechanical issues that she forgot to tell your uncle about." Hicks paused, and out of nowhere said, "My aunt is dead." I went silent. He continued, "She died in this car." Hairs stood up on the back of my neck, and I could feel goosebumps rising on my skin. Then I thought to myself, "He's joking, because he was just telling jokes before the car shut off, and now he's trying to scare us." I waited patiently for him to say that he was just kidding, but it was overshadowed by my friend's silence in the back seat. I broke the silence and asked Hicks to stop kidding around before we were late to the prom, but he remained in silence. I then said, "So, this is your dead aunt's car, and your uncle let you drive his dead wife's car, that she died in to the prom?" "Yeah, right!" He replied, "Yes, it is, and she was found dead in this car not too long ago." My heart began to pound in fear, and from the silence of my friend in the back seat, I could sense that she too was afraid. I asked myself, "Did he plan this?" "Could he be serious?" Hicks then began to tell us about his aunt, and that's when I knew he wasn't kidding around. He first told us about her character, and he said that she was loving and sweet. He then told us how she was found beaten and bloody, and said that the person who did it was never caught. As he continued to tell the story, I eventually connected it to a story that I had heard my mother and grandmother discussing a few weeks earlier. The town was in an uproar because apparently some man had lured his wife to a location and set her up to be brutally murdered. The husband had supposedly called his wife to tell her he had car trouble and asked her to come pick him up. Once she got there, she was attacked and killed by a lady said to be having an affair with the husband. People were saying that the mistress and her grown children committed the crime. I heard my grandmother say that when the man's wife was found; her skull was crushed, eyes gouged out, ears cut off, throat cut, and she was stabbed multiple times. They even discussed what tools were used for the murder, and it was a hammer and a knife. The murder weapons were found; covered in dry blood and wrapped up in an old bloody towel in the attic of a church. The talk was that the smell from the weapons and bloody towel gave away the location and led to the discovery.

    I listened in disbelief as Hicks continued to talk about his aunt, and I couldn't believe that he was connected to the family of the murdered lady. Before now, he had never said anything about her or her funeral. A few days before the prom, I walked in on a conversation between my seamstress neighbor and my mom. I overheard her telling my mom, "You shouldn't let her get involved with that boy and his family because the uncle is strange." When I entered the room she stopped talking, and both refused to say anything further. I didn't understand why she was telling my mom something like that because I had met Hicks's family and his uncles, and they all seemed very nice. But that day, I guess I didn't meet all of them.

Now there I was, sitting in a dead car of a dead woman with the nephew of the man who'd supposedly led her to her death. My mind and pulse were racing just thinking about it. I was nervous and scared, and wanted nothing more than to go home. Hicks seemed nervous and scared too. I didn't know if it was because he knew I was scared and wanted to go home, or if he feared his uncle would blame him for the car. Maybe, he himself had just realized how bad it looked driving the car we were in. I sat shaking in my seat. Hicks got out of the car in to the darkness and tried to look under the hood. He couldn't see well enough to figure out what was wrong, so he closed the hood and got back in. I suggested that we lock the doors, and after we did, we sat in silence. My classmate and I were too afraid to speak, and Hicks were too afraid to speak to me. I prayed that someone would come down the dark road to help us, but no one did.

We sat there for what seemed like hours. Suddenly, the radio turned on, and blasted on its highest level. It almost scared us to death. The car's engine then sprung to life, and it did it without Hicks even turning the ignition. The total darkness was replaced by green light that lit up the car's panel. I looked over at Hicks to find him looking back at me. He had obvious fear in his eyes. The headlights weren't on yet, but soon blinked to life. Hicks didn't say a word, but reached down and put the car in drive, and proceeded down the once dark road. I turned around and looked at my classmate in the back seat, and saw her wide frightened eyes looking back at me, but we said nothing. All three of us remained in complete silence all the way to the prom.

When we got to the prom, all my excitement for the prom had been left on that dark road where the car stalled. I no longer had the desire for festivities because I just wanted to go home. No pictures were taken, no food eaten, we didn't even dance.

My classmate came over and told me that she had gotten herself another way home and said that she didn't want to get back in that car and wouldn't if she were me. Yes, I wanted greatly to catch a ride with someone else, and I think Hicks knew that. Hicks seemed very embarrassed and sad because he knew our prom night had been ruined. For the little bit of time that we were there, I sat on the bleachers staring at him. He stood with his hands in his pockets talking to other friends, and his sad eyes would periodically glance over at me. As I sat there thinking about what had happened with the car and who it belonged to, I became increasingly reluctant to leave with Hicks. He soon approached me and asked if I was ready to leave, and I told him I was. For me, prom night had been an absolute fail, but it wasn't over because I would still have to endure the journey home. I didn't know what I was more afraid of, the car quitting or knowing that a woman lost her life in it.

When we got in the car, Hicks asked if I wanted to go to Alexander City and ride around for a bit. I told him I didn't trust the car because it would probably stall again and make me miss my curfew. He took me home without incident. Once there, he gave me a small peck on the lips, and walked me to my door. After he left, I felt relieved that I was home, but also felt afraid he'd go find another date to help him finish out the ruined prom night. The next day, out of jealousy and curiosity, I asked him. He told me he went home and went to bed, don't know if it was true, but I believed him, and we never discussed what happened that night again; not even with my classmate that witnessed it or with my parents. For the first time, I am choosing to share it with you.

4.

HEAR NO EVIL

I'D STARTED TO FALL FOR HICKS. Even after hearing the terrible things throughout the community about his uncle that I had yet to meet. I still believed that it didn't have anything to do with Hicks. He was such a gentleman, and he was nice and kind. I also refused to believe that the wonderful family I'd met was anything but nice people, so I continued with our relationship.

It was a Sunday, I went to church, and after church Hicks came to see me. We went for a walk and I decided to ask more questions about his aunt. He started to tell me about how sweet she was. He said she was his favorite aunt, and that the family was still grieving her passing. I asked him how his uncle was dealing with the loss. He paused… then started to confide in me about the relationship between his aunt and uncle. He said his uncle was very mean to her, and he made her stay at home all the time while he went out. He told me a sad story about his aunt that he had witnessed. He said one day, his uncle told his aunt to get dressed so they could go visit his sister and his mom. Hicks said his aunt loved his mother and grandmother, and she was so excited about the visit. Hicks said that she hurried and got dressed, but after she was fully dressed, and had entered the room with a big smile on her face, his uncle said, "What are you dressed for, where do you think you're going?" Her smile faded and she said, "You told me to go get dressed, and said that we were going to visit your mom and sister." Hicks then said that his uncle yelled at her and said, "Get out of them clothes because you ain't going nowhere!" Hicks said his aunt dropped her head and left the room crying. He said she cried and cried, and he felt so sorry for her. He said that he hated what his uncle was doing to her, but he was just a kid, so it was nothing he could do or say.

I asked Hicks if he liked going to his uncle's house. He told me that he loved his uncle, and once liked going there until one day his uncle turned on him. He said he was sitting on the floor doing his homework, when his uncle walked by him and snatched his pencil from his hands. He said his uncle broke the pencil in half, and then threw it in the fireplace into a roaring fire. He said his uncle told him to reach his hand in the fire and get the pencil. Hicks said he laughed, and then told his uncle that he wasn't about to reach his hand in the hot fire. He said his uncle's face turned mean, and he began to scream at him; trying to force him to stick his hands in the flames to get the pencil. Hicks said he started crying, but his uncle didn't seem to care. He continued to yell and tell Hicks to get the pencil. Hicks said that he was about ten years old at the time, so he was very afraid. He said that his uncle remained persistent and continued to yell at him. Totally horrified, Hicks said that he bent down and began to reach towards the flames for the pencil. Once he neared the flames, his uncle stopped him and said, "Boy, don't you reach your hands in that fire!" Hicks said that after that incident, he never wanted to go back to his uncle's house again, and when he did go, it was always with another older family member.

Hearing the evil story told by Hicks about his uncle should

have set off warning signals, but again I was naïve, young, and in love. We walked back to my house and sat on the porch and continued to talk about where he came from. While we sat talking, he decided to share another story with me from his childhood. Hicks told me about an old man who lived near them back in the woods where he originally moved from. He said the old man was very scary looking and wore a long black wool coat with a big hood on it. He said that the man would come to their house at night and bring them peanuts and sweet potatoes and would then sit and talk to the adult family members. Hicks said that he and his siblings would peep at him because he looked so scary, but eventually they got used to him because he visited so often. They even started to look forward to the goodies he would bring. Hicks said all a sudden the man stopped coming by, and they wondered where he was. Hicks paused, and became reluctant to finish the story, so I pressured him to finish. After a moment, he started back up and said that months went by and the old man never came back. He said after a year had passed the old man was found. He said some hunters found his coat, and when they lifted it up, the old man's bones were under it.

Hicks paused and looked at me and said, "I shouldn't be telling you this, but everyone said that it was my uncle that robbed and killed the old man." I stared at him but said nothing. I did not ask any more questions because honestly, I was spooked.

Fast forwarding many years later, I would hear another disturbing story about Hicks's uncle from an elderly lady that I assisted. While discussing her childhood, and my family, I found out that she knew Hicks's family too. She told me that growing up, she lived in the same back woods where Hicks's family came from, and her family attended church with them. She said one Sunday after church, the runner; who was a news carrier, ran past her and her little sisters. They followed him to hear the news that he was carrying to her grandparents. She said that the runner reported that a young boy had just been killed on the church grounds, and the killer was a fourteen-year-old boy from the neighborhood who they all knew. She told me the name of the fourteen-year old murderer, and it was Hicks's uncle. The elderly lady went on to say, that the boy, Hicks's uncle, was jealous of the other young boy because he had a job in Alexander City and had money. She said the boy, Hicks's uncle, tried to take the money, and when the boy wouldn't give it to him; they got in to a physical fight. The fourteen-year old boy, Hicks's uncle, then pulled out a butcher's knife and stabbed the boy several times. The boy died, as the church members looked on in horror and disbelief. She told me that Hicks's uncle was arrested, but since he was young; he didn't face any real punishment. She said that he went to jail, but didn't stay in jail long, and it was practically swept under the rug as if it had never happened. She also said that it was possibly overlooked because it was a black person killing another black person, so the authorities didn't care. She also told me that she believed that was when Hicks's uncle got his first taste and thirst for blood.

Sitting on the porch, it had started to get late, so it was time for Hicks to go home. The stories Hicks told me was eerie, but not as eerie as the story he had told me about his aunt because she was now dead, and her death had recently happened, and wasn't solved. After Hicks left, I felt very uneasy. My uneasiness was not because I was afraid of meeting Hicks's uncle, it was because I was afraid that my parents would make me stop seeing Hicks because of his uncle. The next day, I went to my paternal grandmother's house to get more information about the family. I had overheard her saying that she knew Hicks's recently deceased aunt very well, and she said that she had known her for years. When I got there, my grandmother was in the kitchen cooking. She turned and looked at me when I asked her about Hicks's aunt, and I could tell she knew why I was asking. She stared intently at me and said, "She was a very nice lady, and didn't deserve to die the way she did." She gave me the sick details on the condition of the body when it was found. The information terrified me, and it was so bad, I was afraid to walk back home. I could almost visualize it, and I felt an unexplainable gloom. If I felt it, I could only imagine how Hicks and his family must have felt. What I couldn't get past was how horrible her murder was, yet no one had been arrested. Hicks's family was being talked about negatively throughout the community, and yet there I was, totally smitten by the young man connected to that family.

5.

SEE NO EVIL

RUNNING HOME, MANY THOUGHTS ran through my mind. I couldn't shake the thoughts of Hicks's aunt's body the way my grandmother had described it. What was even scarier was that I was running towards an unforeseen fate with Hicks and his family. Would this be the right choice? I should have asked myself that question, but I was blinded by love.

A few days passed before Hicks visited again, and by this time I had graduated from school, and it was about to be out for the summer. Hicks still had a few weeks left of school, and one more year. However, he lost focus because I wasn't there, and dropped out. Hicks became a permanent fixture at my house. My parents and siblings had gotten used to seeing him and loved him. His family had also gotten used to seeing me. Especially, his first cousin and her husband whose truck he used in order to visit me. We were inseparable, if you saw him you saw me, and vice versa.

A year later, I became pregnant. Although Hicks was super excited, I was terrified. I was so terrified that I didn't disclose my pregnancy to my parents and hid it. Hicks and I continued with our relationship and agreed that we'd reveal our secret when the time was right. The night that we decided to tell his first cousin who Hicks often borrowed the truck from, she and her husband were so happy for us. We were at their house when we told them and were all laughing and celebrating. Our celebration was short lived because it was interrupted by a phone call. When Hicks's cousin answered the phone, we all got silent so she could hear the caller. We then heard her scream out, "Oh, Lord have mercy!" "When did that happen?" We sat listening and waiting for her return to the living room to tell us what had happened. I watch Hicks as his confused eyes searched the doorway for his cousin to reappear. She reentered the room with tears streaming down her face and told us that one of their uncles had been found dead. Hicks immediately jumped up, and he and his cousin and her husband readied themselves to head to the family house. I asked them to take me home, so they did. I didn't hear from Hicks for two or three days, but the news of his uncle's death had spread throughout our small community, and it was another mysterious death.

The night Hicks's uncle was found dead, I will never forget the weather. It was a dreary night, misty and foggy. It never rained, it just kept drizzling. It was said that Hicks's uncle's body was found next to a church face down in a mud puddle. It was said that he was intoxicated when he fell in, so he drowned. I'd only met him once during my first visit to Hicks's house, but I remember him smiling and telling me that I was pretty. Hicks would talk about him often, and I could tell that he was his favorite uncle. The day I met him, he seemed like a very nice man. He was tall and thin with very beautiful brown eyes. He was quite handsome, and had an infectious laugh, and everyone seemed to love him. People in the community described him as a nice man who was quiet and kept to himself. This community was also saying that they believed he was murdered and believed that it was done by his brother. Even the local newspaper started writing stories about the deaths, and they were questioning why death seemed to be visiting the same family, and so frequently, and they also wanted to know why the murders were not being solved.

I wanted to be there for Hicks but did not want to attend the funeral. I felt bad for him and his family, and I was sad that they were connected to such horrible tragedies. Hicks stayed away for about two days, and then on the third day he came to see me. I could tell from his appearance that the death of his uncle had hurt him deeply, and it had taken a toll on him. His uncle's death had changed him physically, and to me he looked older. His uncle lived in the same house with him, and he had told me that they slept in the same sleeping quarters of his house. Hicks had always been happy go lucky, and his energy and charisma is what I believe attracted me to him. Now, he seemed sad and reserved, and to me he looked puzzled. I could tell from his silence, he was questioning things in his head, but would not share his thoughts with me. I'd already heard the circulated stories, and knew why he seemed withdrawn and puzzled, and the community was puzzled too.

The night Hicks's uncle was found face down in a puddle, it had not rained but drizzled, and so everyone was wondering how a drowning could happen. I myself wondered how a grown man could lay face down in a puddle without attempting to get up or roll out of it. I like others had my suspicions; especially since I had overheard my mother and dad discussing the incident. She told my dad that she had driven past the church which was down the road from where Hicks's uncle was found. She said she was on her way home, and as she passed the church, she saw Hicks's uncle's car parked there. My dad said he believed the death was no accident, and he heard many other say the same.

My dad then warned my mom that she should be careful who she talked to about what she saw, and he told her to watch her surroundings just in case Hicks's uncle saw her. The death scene and scenario were a lie, but since no one spoke up, it was ruled an accidental drowning…another incident many believed was made to look like an accident.

Hicks sat staring into space on my porch, and to me he looked like a lost child. I really didn't know what to say to him but knew how he felt since I had lost two uncles myself. At the time, I really couldn't comfort him because I was more worried about my situation, and that was the unborn child growing in my belly. I knew I'd have to eventually come clean and tell my parents, but I still wasn't ready. Not only that, I knew they'd be concerned about me being locked into a family where everyone seemed to be dying off. These thoughts consumed me, and it was a terrible feeling that would only get worse.

6.

Do No Evil

THE BIBLE SAYS, "Do unto others as you would have them do unto you." Even though Hicks's uncle was a preacher, he did not abide by this rule. He would also not abide by the rule "Love thy neighbor as thyself" or "Covet not their neighbor's house." Hicks's uncle's wife had been dead only a few months when he set his eyes upon a new woman. The woman he chose was married to his next-door neighbor. Since Hicks's uncle was no longer being investigated for murder, he became bold. He was the community boogie man and became untouchable. Many believed he was powerful and was getting his powers from black magic. Talk circulated that he was deeply involved in voodoo and made frequent visits to a tribe of sisters called the Seven Sisters. The Seven Sisters was said to have supplied him potions and spells. Today, if you Google the name Seven Sisters, you'll be able to pull up information on the company. Once you access it, you'll be able to order all sorts of spells and potions over the Internet. No one had ever seen the Seven Sisters, but it was said that Hicks's uncle would make constant trips to Birmingham to visit them. On one particular visit to the sisters, he supposedly bought a deadly potion. This potion was said to be used to kill his neighbor, so he could have his wife.

The neighbor and his wife were a beautiful couple and had two beautiful sons. My mom knew him and his family well, and I heard her talk about how nice looking he was. I think she even had a slight infatuation with him. She once told me that she thought he was well maintained; whatever that meant. It was a shock to my mom and others when that young man became deathly ill, and no one knew what was wrong with him. My mom visited his family, and they said that the doctors that tried to treat him could not diagnose his condition. Eventually, the young man lost his ability to speak, and people that visited him said that his body had become twisted like a vine. The man, Hicks's uncle's neighbor, lingered in this condition for almost a year. A family friend was there visiting one day, when he witnessed Hicks's uncle's visit to the man. He said the man went in to a fit when Hicks's uncle walked in. The family friend said that he and the man's wife couldn't calm him down, and he wouldn't calm down until after Hicks's uncle left the house.

The young man lived about a year after his illness. They said on the day he died, he had eaten cabbage that was given to his wife by Hicks's uncle, and he died shortly after eating it. A short time after the young man's death, Hicks's uncle and the next-door neighbor's widow were married, and a few months later she gave birth to his child. The death of the young man was never investigated, but again the community talked about the speedy marriage of his widow, and the quick birth of the child for her new husband. My mom was very upset by the death of the young man and was even more upset about how fast his wife had moved on.

I finally got to meet the widow of the young man, but she was now the wife of Hicks's uncle. I met her one day while visiting his family. She was beautiful, and smart. She also had a very shapely figure, and I noticed that when she walked, she would strut like a model. She was articulate, and I could tell that she was educated. When Hicks's uncle married her, I was only nineteen at the time, and I believe that she was in her late twenties' early thirties. I never really had any real conversation with her other than saying hello and goodbye, but I loved listening to her talk, and I admired her. However, I thought of her as a fool for marrying Hicks's uncle and giving him a baby; especially since there was so much controversy about the death of his first wife. However, I knew that I couldn't be too judgmental of her because just like her, I was locking myself into the same family, and I was only a few months away from giving birth myself.

I still hadn't told my parents that Hicks and I were expecting a baby, and since I was not showing, I held on to my secret a little longer. Hicks and I knew that with an arrival of a baby we would need to have an income. We discussed that we would have to go and get jobs, and this would cushion my situation, and help our parents see that we were going to be responsible parents. I personally, hoped a job would lessen my parents' wrath. We drove to the local textile mill and applied, and a couple of days later we were both notified that we'd gotten the job. Once Hicks told his mother that he had gotten a job, she bought him a car. It was a little red GTO that he'd seen sitting beside the road with a for sale sign on it. At the textile mill, we were placed on different shifts, and it worked out well because he could pick me up and drop me off each day. I worked ten a.m. to six p.m., and Hicks worked from six a.m. to two p.m. I couldn't drive, so Hicks started teaching me how to drive on the weekends because he wanted me to be able to keep the car once our baby came. His car was a stick shift, and after a few weekends of drive time, I caught on. I would keep the car and drive wherever I needed to go, but without a license. I got my first ticket at age twenty for speeding, so this prompted me to go get one. I continued working, saving and preparing. Since, I had transportation and was working, I started going to the doctor. After several months without prenatal care, I was happy to know that my baby was healthy and progressing well, but I continued to keep my pregnancy a secret.

Finally, I started to show. I was almost nine months and could no longer hide my full belly, so I was forced to tell my parents. Hicks and I told them together, and it didn't go over well at all. My dad tried to whip me, and we ended up in a standoff because I wouldn't let him. I knew he didn't realize how far along I was. My mom had to calm him down, and she reminded him, that I was older than she was when he had gotten her pregnant. However, it didn't stop her from telling me how angry and disappointed she was in me. Hearing this made me sad, and I felt bad about letting her down. I was basking in self-pity until I realized; I had practically raised all their children, so I was the one who should have been disappointed. After this realization, I began to celebrate my pregnancy, and for the first time in my life, I would finally have something of my own. Plus, Hicks and I both had jobs, so we weren't asking them for anything.

A few weeks later, our daughter arrived. The morning my water broke, I kept having a reoccurring dream that Hicks's sister kept saying the word milk, and after she did, I would have to get up and go pee. When I would lie back down the dream would pick up where it left off, and she would say the word again, and I would have to immediately get up and go pee again. I don't remember the context of how she said it, but remembered begging her in my dream to stop, and when I would, she would laugh and say the word again. Eventually, the desire to pee became contractions, and I had to wake my parents up to have them take me to the hospital. They took me to Tuskegee, and I gave birth there. Hicks was at work when he was told and went around the neighborhood begging someone to ride with him to the hospital because he didn't know how to get there. No one would, so he couldn't be there for the birth of our daughter. However, when we got home from the hospital, he showed up with bells on.

When Hicks entered the house, I was sitting on the couch and the baby was lying beside me under a blanket. When he came in to the house, he was so busy staring at me on the couch he didn't even realize that the baby was next to me under the blanket. In fact, he almost sat down on her, but my mom screamed at him and said, "Don't sit on that baby!" He literally stopped himself in midair and stood back up. He turned and looked down at the blanket and stared at it. I had the baby covered, and only a little of her hair was peeking out from under it. He stared at the little mound covered by the blanket then slowly removed it. The removal of the blanket caused the baby to flinch and move.

He continued to un-wrapped her with tears in his eyes. I think he was also hurt by the thought that he almost plopped down on her. He picked her up and sat down with her and gazed at her as if she was a new species. From that moment on, he fell completely in love with our baby. Hicks was different than most fathers who had little girls because he took her with him almost every time, he left the house. I was replaced with a new girl, and now if you saw him, you saw her instead of me. He would come by and grab our daughter and her hairbrush and take her around town to visit different family members to show her off. When he sat still, he would sit brushing her hair and watching it re-curl. She had a lot of hair, and he would sit and create different little curly styles. He brushed her hair so much and so often that I had to get on to him. I guess this was his way of bonding with her.

I don't know who loved my daughter more: me, Hicks, or my parents and siblings. She was the first child, grandchild, and niece. My family treated her as if she belonged to them, and I practically had to sneak her away, so that Hicks's family could spend some time with her too. You couldn't tell my sister, who was two years younger than me, that my daughter wasn't hers. As time went on, my daughter became really attached to her too, and would cry if my sister even left the room. Hicks's, family loved the baby too. She was not the first grandchild, but she was the first granddaughter, so she was spoiled on both ends. When we would take my daughter to visit Hicks's mom, we would constantly get lectures about getting married. Hicks's, mom would bring it up the second I got there, and in every conversation. She would almost be in tears and would say that she didn't want her grand-daughter to be a bastard baby. Marriage meant so much to her; even though she had Hicks's older brother and younger sister out of wedlock. She married Hicks's father and gave him three children before divorcing him, so she had five kids in all.

Hicks's, mom finally wore us down, and six months later we decided to get married. We were married at the local courthouse instead of having a formal church ceremony. The day we took our vows, our daughter went with us, and crawled around on the courthouse floor. However, the day before Hicks and I got married, my dad called me in to his bedroom and had a private talk with me. He told me that I didn't have to marry Hicks if I didn't want to. He said, "I know you have a baby, but you don't have to marry him just because you have one, and if you don't wanna, you don't have to." At that time, and looking at him, I know he was saying this to me because he was afraid for me. He was worried and was concerned about my entrance into the family that he had heard so many disturbing things about one of its members. However, I assured him that I wanted to marry Hicks, and that I was happy. I never told him about feeling pressured by Hicks's mom. Plus, I loved Hicks, and believed that we would have married eventually anyway. Hicks and I were young parents that were still very much in love, and I believed that everything was going to be okay, and I had no doubt that it wouldn't be, so I went ahead and married him.

After our courthouse wedding, we went and informed his mom. We surprised her with our news, and I remember his sister inviting us to her house to celebrate. She prepared a feast for us, and we spent the day with her and her husband. Our future was going to be bright, and I loved my new in-laws. Plus, no one in Hicks's family had died in a while, so everything seemed o.k. However, the spirit of my marriage and new family was short lived. Two weeks after my wedding, and two weeks and one day after the conversation with my dad; death would visit Hicks's family again, but now it was my family too.

The morning before the new tragedy, Hicks picked me up from work like he always did. On the way down the road, I told him how I wished a liquor store was open because I really needed a drink to unwind. Hicks said, "I got something." He then pulled a small pint of clear liquid from his glove compartment that didn't have a label. I assumed it was vodka or gin. I was shocked when I saw him with the bottle because I knew he really didn't drink, and when he did there was always more soda than alcohol in his beverage. He couldn't even finish a beer. However, I was glad he had it. I asked him to pass it to me so I could take a drink from it. Hicks looked at me and said, "I can't give you none of this." I asked him why not, and his response was, "I just can't." Then he opened it and took a small drink from it then topped it up and put it back into his glove compartment. I asked him if he had gotten the pint from his uncle, and he wouldn't respond. I quietly shook my head at him, folded my arms, and sat in silence and looked at the road, as his headlights illuminated the lines on it. I wanted my silence to indicate that I was disappointed at his refusal to share, but he ignored my silent treatment, and continued down the road; matching my silence.

All the sudden, Hicks's car began to chime. When Hicks looked down at his indicators, he said that the noise was his gas light alert. I asked him if he had enough to make it to my parent's house. He answered, "Maybe, but I don't want to take that chance." We stopped at a service station that was on Highway Number Nine. The service station wasn't opened yet, and it was right below his uncle's house. We parked near a tank and waited for it to open. Hicks was always almost on empty any time we went somewhere. The main reason was because he was notorious for souping up his engine and driving fast, so his gas tank was always low or empty. I constantly stayed on his case about this because I was often left sitting in his car on the side of the road somewhere; waiting for him to come back with fifty cents worth of gas.

We both sat staring into the darkness as we waited. Hicks knew I was still angry about the alcohol as well as his failure to make sure his car had enough gas, so he kept quiet. However, sitting still was not his strong suit because Hicks was a very impatient person, and I've noticed that most people under the Aries Zodiac sign often are, and this now includes my daughter who is also under this sign and very impatient. Not only was Hicks impatient, he was always restless, and that morning was no different. Hicks grabbed his flashlight, got out of the car, and opened the hood. He started examining and working on a car that had no issues like always. While he was out there, I watched as light from his flash light glimmered through the slits of his open hood. There was faint light behind the car, so I turned in its direction. It was coming from one big street light that was located up the road from his uncle's house. When I turned back around, I caught a glimpse of something coming up the highway. It was a pack of dogs. I didn't see where they had come from, but they were heading up the highway in our direction. I rolled my window down, and in a low excited whisper said, "Hicks, Hicks, get in the car!" I just knew that the dogs were on their way to attack him. He came to the window, and asked, "What do you want?" I pointed in the direction of the dogs, and I told him to look at them. He looked in their direction without concern. He didn't move from my window, and we both watched the dogs trot past us; never giving us a look or second thought. When they neared Hicks's uncle's house, they stopped in the road and howled under the dim light. Hicks and I continue to watch the dogs as their howls became moans, and it almost sounded as if they were weeping. Hicks never moved, and I couldn't move. After a few moments of howling, moaning, and weeping in front of the house, the dogs headed on up the road. When I turned back to look at Hicks, he was already leaning down into my window and was looking at me. He said, "I bet you think they're howling over there at my uncle's house, don't you?" I responded and said, "You see them, and you know what house they're howling at." He didn't say a word and went back to the hood of his car. Not long after, the store owner pulled up and we were able to get gas and go home.

The next day, the beautiful, smart, and shapely woman who strutted like a model was found dead in her car. The second wife of Hicks's uncle appeared to have been in a car accident. The people on the scene said it appeared to be a minor accident because the car was resting on a small bush without much damage. Authorities said that there was no way that she could have died from the incident. When Hicks came to tell me the news about his uncle's wife, his eyes were red and swollen. I could tell that he had been crying and was scared out of his mind. I could also tell that he didn't want to tell me what happened because he knew what we both had seen the morning before. He told me that he went to the scene when the family got the word and watch as they brought his aunt's car back to the highway. He said when he got there she was still in the car. He told me that when they removed her from the car and placed her body on the gurney, she began to bloat and swell. He said she was blowing up like a balloon, and suddenly, her skin began to split as if invisible knives were cutting it. He stopped and looked at me and searched my eyes for my thoughts, but I didn't give him a clue to what I was thinking. I simply hugged him and told him how sorry I was. I could feel him relax in my arms, and he hugged me back. We quietly sat holding each other on my parents' porch for what seemed like forever. I could tell that he didn't want to go home, but after a while he got up, and told me that he'd be back later to see our daughter and left. When the rest of the community found out about the death, people started talking. Word even got around that someone had seen Hicks's uncle that night in his wife's car. They said that when they saw him, he was partially turned in his seat, and it looked like he was hitting something in the back seat, and the car was even swerving as he did.

Some years later, a trusted friend who was also one of my teachers, revealed to me that Hicks's uncle's second wife showed up at her house the night before she was found dead. She said she was beating on her front door begging to be let in. The teacher said her husband opened the door as she stood behind him. She said the second wife barely let the door open before she pushed her way through. The teacher told me that she was crying hysterically when she came in and was begging for help. The teacher told me she said, "Help me!" "Please call the police, please!" "He's going to kill me!" The teacher said that she was dirty, and her hair was all over her head. She said her clothes were ripped, and she was shoeless. She said that she and her husband were both so afraid they didn't know what to do. She told me they tried to calm her down so they could get more information, but before she could get a word out; they heard pounding knocks coming from the front door. She said the knocks frightened all of them. Her husband opened the door, and when he did, they saw Hicks's uncle standing there. He then demanded that his wife come out of the house and go with him. The teacher went on to say that the wife did as he instructed, and she believe she did it to protect them. I asked the teacher why she didn't help by at least calling the police. She responded, "I was too frightened, I just wanted them out of my house because I had my own family to think about." She went on to say, how heartbroken she was when they got the news the next day about the wife's death, and she said that I was the only person she had confided in about what happened because her husband had told her never to tell anyone, and to just stay out of it, and she did what he said.

Later, I got more information while visiting Hicks first cousin who had visited the uncle's house earlier that afternoon before the death. She told me she had just gotten out of the hospital with yellow jaundice, and she and her sister had decided to stop by their uncle's house to visit his wife. She said that when they got there, they heard screams coming from inside of the house, so they ran to the porch. When they got on the porch the door was open and the screen door was locked, so they looked through it. She told me her and her sister saw their uncle viciously punching his wife as she tried to protect her face. They watched in disbelief through the screen door then they knocked. She said he stopped and looked toward the open door, and said, "I'm busy, yawl come back later!" She told me his wife was down on the floor while he was still straddled over her. She said they walked away with their hearts pounding in their chests because he looked like a wild man. The cousin told me her sister dropped her off and she went on home. At the time, she was dropped off at the family house, and stayed there to lie down and rest because she was not fully recovered, nor feeling her best. She told me early that next morning about four or five a.m., she woke up to find her uncle standing over her in the early dawn of the morning. She said he scared her half to death. She told me that he asked her, "You just got out of the hospital because you are sick, right?" She said that she responded, "Uncle, you know I am sick." He then said to her, "You better stay that way then!" She said after he said this, he turned around and left out of her room leaving her shocked and filled with fear. I asked her had she told anyone else, and she told me that she had not because she was scared. Out of curiosity, I then asked her why she told me. She just shrugged her shoulders and didn't answer. To this day, I believe she told me in case something happened to her later, so there could be a clue.

7.

MOTHERLESS CHILD

AFTER THE DEATH AND BURIAL of Hicks's uncle's beautiful second wife, everyone felt terrible for the little boys she had left behind; especially the child that was almost two years old. Talk throughout the community was that Hicks's uncle was committing these murders for money. It was said that he was taking out insurance policies on his family members and would collect once they died. But, after hiring accomplices, paying attorney fees, and buying expensive cars, and living a certain lifestyle, he had to kill again to generate more income.

After a few months of going back and forth to my parents, Hicks moved us into the family house. He said it would be just until we could get our own place. He had grown tired of coming so far to see our daughter and picking me up for work and dropping me off. While I was there, I would daily see Hicks's uncle. He would come there to drop off his little son. We all noticed that the little boy began to get sick. His body soon started to break out in pus filled sores, and eventually the sores covered his entire body. He even had crusty sores on his eye lids. I watched the concern of the family, and I was concerned too because my daughter was there. The sores would constantly ooze clear fluid, and the pain from them made him cry all the time.

He was about two years old, and I felt so sorry for him.

Eventually, Hicks's uncle left the little boy with his aging mother and Hicks's mom full time so they could care for him, but he was never totally out of the picture. The sores had gotten so bad that they had even spread to the palms of his hands. My daughter was almost fifteen months old, and I tried my best to keep her away from him because I didn't want her to get what he had. It was hard because I would get constant knocks on my locked bedroom door by the little boy, asking to play with "baby sister". I would refuse his visits and pretend that I was sleep, but my locked door would be opened by Hicks's grandmother. I don't know how, but she could get through any locked door in the house, and she would come in and confiscate "Baby Sister;" the name even she called my daughter after being given it by her young grandson. I would be livid because he always wanted to play with her, and I didn't want him to because no one seemed to know what was wrong with him.

Although the little boy was covered in sores, his father never took him to the doctor, and I don't remember anyone else taking him. However, he'd bring him medicine in jugs that looked like clear water. He would then tell his mother that it was medicine, and that she needed to put it on his sores. I remember listening to him from the bedroom; telling his mother to wash his son's sores with the clear solution. When his mother would use the clear fluid, it would burn the little boy, and you could hear his screams all through the house. I felt that the medicine wasn't helping him, it seemed to make the sores worst. I couldn't understand why his mother couldn't understand that, but I kept quiet and continued to watch. I simply couldn't understand why she allowed him to keep bringing the regimen that only made the little boy sicker, and again, it didn't have any labeling on it to even tell anyone what it was.

Eventually, his mother got fed up with her son because he would never explain what the medicine was, or where he had gotten it, so she stopped using it and went to a home remedy to cure her grandson. I remember the day she went into the woods and gathered the herbs. She called it Ardi Tag. The herb had red berries on it, and she said that she retrieved it from a tree limb. I watched as she boiled, strained, and added sugar to it. She gave him a portion of this concoction every day, and the sores eventually began to dry up and slowly heal. Hicks's uncle also saw that his son was getting well, but instead of being glad, he began to get angry. I heard him ask his mom whether or not she was still using the medicine that he was providing, and his mother told him that she was. She then told him that his son was getting better, so to just let her handle it. I listened as Hicks's uncle raised his voice at her and told her that he was about to take his son to the doctor. She yelled back and asked why he wanted to take him to the doctor now that he could see that his son was getting better. He told her he just thought it was best, and that it was time for him to take him to see a real doctor.

He grabbed up his son while his mom and Hicks's mom begged him not to take him. He grabbed up the boy and left with him. He stayed gone for a long time, and I listen as the family discussed the boy and talked about how worried they were about him. I came out of my room and saw terror in everyone's face, but I acted like I didn't know what was going on. A few hours later, Hicks's uncle returned with the little boy. He was crying and in excruciating pain. So much so, it made Hicks grandmother cry, and she kept asking her son to explain what had happened. Hicks's uncle answered, "Aw, ain't nothing wrong with him, he just wants to have a crying spell, he's alright." He then passed his son to his mom, turned and went out of the door, and soon I saw him leaving in his car. The little boy continued to wail in pain, as the family looked on scared and confused. I even tried to calm him, but he wouldn't stop crying. Hicks's, grandmother rubbed and consoled the little boy, and then gave him some more of her home remedy. After she administered her medicine, the child fell asleep. But, when he woke up, the sores were back to oozing pus again. I felt terrible watching the little boy go through so much. He was just a little bit older than my daughter, and I couldn't imagine her being so sick and in so much pain. After that day, Hicks grandmother would no longer allow her son to take the little boy. She guarded over him with her life, and day by day he got better and eventually healed.

Since the little boy did not die as planned, another plot was formed. This time, the plot would be to kill his two step sons from his second marriage. This plot was revealed by one of his henchmen who at the time had too much to drink and confided in someone while they were intoxicated. The henchmen told his drink server that he declined the offer because he couldn't be responsible for hurting children. With the offer declined, now there would have to be a new victim.

8.
HICKS

SOMETIME LATER, HICKS AND I moved from his family home into our own cozy little home with our daughter. I had returned to work because now my daughter could talk and walk and was old enough to be left with a baby sitter. One of Hicks's cousins babysat her, and it was convenient because it was walking distance from our home.

Shortly after we moved into our home, Hicks began to act strange. He constantly left the house without saying goodbye; never letting me know where he was going, nor when he was coming back, and we would argue about this. I remember one day he was getting dressed to leave the house, and I asked him where he was about to go, and he wouldn't tell me. We got into an argument that escalated into a shoving match. I then hauled off and slapped him, and he slapped me right back and left the house. He wasn't gone long, but when I saw him coming back home. I ran to the kitchen and put ketchup around my mouth to pretend that it was blood. I laid down on the floor near the door and pretended that I was knocked out. When Hicks entered the door, he immediately said, "Won't you get up from there because I can smell that ketchup!" I did but remained angry with him. He had never shown me any kind of violence, but he showed me that day that if I put my hands on him, he would reciprocate.

Hicks didn't like confrontation, and he would leave before he argued with you. He saw that I was still in my feelings, so he walked back out of the door and started working on his car paying my anger no attention. Hicks was sweet as can be, but he had a temper that matched mine, if I pushed his buttons. Again, he wasn't big on arguing, and if he saw that I was mad at him, he would defuse my anger by staying outside or away from me. His refuge was always outside working on a car that wasn't broken, and when he broke it, he fixed it.

Time rocked on, and we were in our small house for almost a year. I continued to notice how Hicks was changing. Before, we would always have deep conversation and would talk for hours. But now, he had become very secretive, and would no longer confide in me or tell me anything. His first love was his daughter, and then his car, and there wasn't really any room for anything else. Just like his daughter, his love for his car was known throughout the community, and he loved to drive it very fast. He soon stopped focusing on safety, and I began to notice that his driving had become even more erratic, so much so, I began to fear riding with him.

One Saturday, we dropped our daughter off at his mother's, and we went shopping for groceries. We were on our way back home, just a few blocks from our house when Hicks stopped at a two way stop on Highway Number Nine. He looked both ways, and so did I. Coming up the road was a semi-truck carrying a load of cars. Hicks sat there, I assumed waiting for it to pass, but when it got to us, he pulled out in front of it. The driver of the semi was on his horn, and I could hear the truck's breaks squealing out along with my screams. The next thing I heard was the metal colliding, and the semi-truck struck my side of the car. It hit the space between my door and the hood, and once it did, it started to spin us like a tornado in the middle of the road. We were spinning right in front of the oncoming semi, and before our car could fully straighten, it was hit a second time on the trunk area of the car instead of head on. The force flung us to the side of the road, and there the car came to a rest.

When I finally convinced myself to stop screaming, I sat there in disbelief that we were alive. Neither one of us got a scratch on us, but I could immediately feel the soreness in my muscles from tensing up before and after the impact. Hicks GTO car was completely totaled. I peered out the side window to see bent and mangled metal looking back at me. When I tried to move, I noticed that my neck and shoulders were stiff, so I quickly grabbed the review mirror, and used it to look back at the semi and its driver. Instead of immediately seeing the truck or the driver, I saw Hicks's uncle parked down the road a few feet from our accident, and he appeared to be watching us from his car. This seemed strange to me because he had gotten there before any police or paramedics. Hicks immediately opened his door and jumped out of our wrecked car, and he went and got in to his uncle's car. He didn't even go and check on the man that we had hit, nor did the man that hit us come to check on us; he remained in his semi. Hicks stayed in his uncle's car, and the man stayed in his semi until the state troopers came. I sat in the car alone shaking while my muscles had spasms. I was sitting there basically in shock when someone from our community stopped and asked if I was okay. I told them I was and asked if they could give me a ride home. Once they got me to my house, I asked them if they could take me to my parent's house. They agreed and waited while I entered my house and packed a few things for myself and my daughter. We had to pass back by the accident, and by that time a State Trooper was there, and Hicks was standing on the side of the highway talking to him. Hicks looked as if he was explaining what happened, and I noticed that his uncle was still there watching from his car. Hicks never even saw me pass, but I noticed another thing, the man in the semi was not out there with them and was still sitting in his truck.

When I got to my parent's house, I busted through the door, and through tears told what happened. My dad wasn't there, but my mom was, and she got very upset. When my dad got home, both called me in to their room and talked to me. Together, they told me that they weren't going to let me go back home to my house and told me not to even try. A few minutes later my dad noticed that my daughter wasn't there. He immediately told me and my mom to go get her. When my mom and I got to Hicks's mom's house, my mom stayed in the car while I went in to get my daughter. Hicks's, mom seemed surprised to see me back so soon, and told me that she was looking forward to keeping her granddaughter overnight. She seemed as if she was waiting for me to tell her that her granddaughter could stay, but when I didn't, she went and retrieved her from a back bedroom where she had been taking a nap. She looked disappointed when she was passing her to me.

My conversation with her was minimal. I tried not to let on that anything was wrong, but she could sense it. When she asked, I told her that I was o.k., and took my daughter's things from her hand. I was going to let her son be the one to tell her that he pulled out in front of a semi and totaled the car that she had bought for him. As I walked out the door to my dad's car, I heard Hicks's mom calling me, but I pretended like I didn't hear her, and got on in the car and left. I knew that she was calling me because she noticed that I had originally dropped off the baby with Hicks but was leaving with the baby in my dad's car.

After a few hours, Hicks went home, and noticed that I wasn't there. He immediately went to his mom's house, and saw that our daughter wasn't there, and was told that I had picked her up. He showed up at my parent's house, and that's when I told him that I wasn't ever going back to our home with him. He was devastated, and he showed up every day there after trying to talk me in to coming back home. He was literally begging, but I wouldn't budge. He knew why I didn't want to come home but tried to convince me that I was over-reacting and it was just a car accident. He even tried to guilt me in to believing that I was breaking up our family, and said that if I stayed, he was taking our daughter with him. I knew that he knew that wasn't going to happen, but I guess he thought it was worth a try.

A few weeks later, Hicks had gotten another car, and it was just as nice as the one he wrecked. He came to my parent's house in it, and when I saw it, I asked him where he'd gotten it from. He told me that his uncle had gotten it for him. Suspicious, I asked him, "Why did your uncle buy you a car?" Hicks answered and said, "He had promised me a car a long time ago, and me and my brother was supposed to have gone to Birmingham to pick it up, but for some reason he changed his mind until now, so this is the car he promised me." I just looked at him, and I could tell that he believed his uncle was just keeping his promise. Even as naïve as I was, I knew that you couldn't get something for nothing, and knew that it would eventually cost Hicks something, but I just didn't know what. I knew Hicks's uncle knew he needed another car because hell, he was on the scene after our accident. But what I wanted to know, was why did he feel obligated to get him one. Hicks quickly changed the subject, and then told me to go in and get our daughter, and our stuff, so we could go home. I looked at him as if I was talking to someone deaf, and leaned into his face and told him, "No!" He tried to ask me to lower my voice, so my parents and sibling wouldn't hear our discussion, but I showed him that it didn't matter who heard what because the answer was still going to be no. After a couple of hours of pleading his case with no success, he got up and left.

The next day, Hicks came to see me, but I was not there. My siblings told him that I had gone to the store with our parents. Hicks asked my siblings how long we'd been gone, and when they told him, he went to his car and headed in our direction. He caught up to us and turned in before my dad could even turn off the ignition. He got out of the car, and in front of my parents began to beg and plead without shame for me to come back home. I gave him the same answer which was no. This day, my no angered Hicks. He returned to his car, got in, and drove to the edge of the highway and waited for traffic to pass. After several cars passed, he continued to sit there, so my parents and I continued to watch him. We saw a logging truck coming down the road, and when it was almost to Hicks, he pulled out right in front of it as if he was trying to commit suicide. The truck was on its horn and breaks trying not to hit him, and if Hicks wouldn't have pulled off on to the shoulder of Highway Number Nine, he would have been pulverized by the huge truck. I remember screaming out, "Oh God!" I watched in horror, as my parents stood there and watched in disbelief. After the truck passed Hicks, he got back on the road and sped down the highway on the tail of the truck that had just almost hit him. My dad finally spoke and said, "Did you see that shit?" Then he turned to me and said, "You need to stay away from them people." Now, my dad was lumping him in with his uncle, and this made me sad. My mom then spoke and said, "That fool just almost got killed." I was so embarrassed.

It started to seem as if Hicks had a death wish. Every time you saw him, he was on the side of the road being ticketed. Our local police who was the husband of our seamstress neighbor had ticketed him on several occasions for speeding and told me he did it to help him because he didn't want him to get hurt or hurt someone else. One day, while I and others were at the laundry mat, we heard a big commotion with sirens blaring and blue lights flashing. Everyone ran from the laundry mat to see what was going on. When I looked out, there stood Hicks being ticketed by our local cop again. He would pay his tickets, and before you know it, he would have another one. I wouldn't be surprised even to this day, if Hicks has a ticket on file that he didn't get a chance to pay.

After several incidents, Hicks finally calmed down. He knew he had to change his ways for me to come back. I don't think he was expecting me and our daughter to be gone for as long as we were, so he made the necessary changes for me to go back. However, I told him that I didn't want to go back to our original house because I vowed that I wouldn't return there. Together, we rented another small house, and believe it or not we were happy. We were getting along very well, and although we had spent some time being separated, we picked back up on the happier parts of our relationship. My parents were leery, but they didn't intervene. We both continued to maintain our jobs and provided for our daughter. Our shifts were still the same. Hicks was on second shift, and I was still on third, so when I would get home I would sleep because my shift required me to be up all night, and so he would watch our baby.

One morning, I awoke to voices outside of our house, and I laid there listening to the elevated voice over a small trembling voice. I tried to figure out who the voices belonged to but couldn't. I got up and peeped out of my door and saw Hicks's uncle standing over him talking down to him in our yard. That day, I saw Hicks in a new light, and that was as a weak man who was afraid of his uncle. I went to the front door and saw that it was open, so I peered out through the screen. I saw my daughter on her toy near the disagreement, and she was closer to the highway than she should have been, and that scared me. If my daughter had ventured off, I don't believe Hicks would have even seen her because his uncle had his full attention. All I could hear Hicks saying was, "O.k. uncle, o.k. uncle, I'm going to do it." Hicks's, voice continued to tremble, and it sounded as if he was close to tears. To break his uncle's spell, I yelled out the door and called Hicks name. His uncle had him in a trance, but when Hicks heard me, I saw that I startled him, and he quickly turned to look at me. His uncle turned and looked at me too and gave me a long evil stare. I looked back at him with that same evil stare that went on for a few seconds, and then I placed my hands on my hips to let him know that I wasn't afraid of him and wasn't moving from the door. I then asked Hicks, "Where is your daughter?" I could see our daughter but wanted to snap him back to reality. I saw a panicky look on Hicks face as he quickly scanned the yard to see our daughter who was on the side of him playing. I could tell he had forgotten all about her. I then yelled out at him, "You better not let her get away from you, and get out there in that highway, and get hit by a car!" When I said this, he went and picked her up as his uncle watched. His uncle glanced back at me a final time, and then walked to his car and left.

Hicks's, uncle's visits to our house became constant and relentless. He wasn't afraid of me at all and wanted me to know that. He seemed to always visit when he knew I was sleeping, and I would always awake to find him in our yard. Hicks and I began to argue, and this made our marriage rocky again. I told Hicks that I was tired of his uncle's unscheduled visits and constant interference in our life. The arguments got more and more severe, and it was almost as if his uncle knew this and would pop up even more.

One morning during an argument, Hicks anger got the better of him, and he revealed his uncle's plot to kill me. We were arguing about him starting to change again, and I told him I was going to leave with our daughter, if he didn't act right. I also told him that I was also going to leave if he didn't make his uncle stay away from our house so much. My statement made him snap and he said, "Keep on, and my uncle is going to burn you up in this house while you're sleeping!" Hicks's, statement should have made me run for the hills because I knew his uncle was associated with other unsolved incidents, but I shooed it off and told Hicks that I wasn't studying him or his crazy ass uncle, and I went on about my business. In fact, I went to work and came home several nights, and went to sleep at our house. However, I no longer slept soundly like I once did. Although I told Hicks I wasn't studying him or his uncle, in the back of my mind I was, and knew I had to be careful.

Hicks must have told his uncle what I said because he started to limit his visits and popups, and later started showering Hicks with gifts. Hicks would come into the house excited saying, "Look what my uncle gave us!" The gifts would be things for our house like curtains, bedspreads, and he even gave us a radio.

Although the gifts were nice, I was just happy that Hicks's uncle was finally treating him nice. Hicks seemed more relaxed to, and we were getting along again.

Time rolled on, and suddenly Hicks's uncle started appearing again. It was after Hicks had somehow acquired another nice car. It was a beautiful red sports car; I believe a Firebird. The day he brought the car home, I remember standing in my window and seeing two cars come up the driveway. In one car was Hicks, and in the second car was his uncle. I watched as the two got out of their cars and began a conversation in our front yard. I noticed that Hicks's uncle had assumed that same domineering position and was standing directly in his face telling him something. I listened to his uncle's tone, and it sounded as if he was giving commands. His voice sounded as if it was rumbling and growling. Hicks's uncle then returned to his car, and instead of turning around and driving out of our driveway like he usually did, he backed completely out of it, and then headed up the road. Hicks stood there watching him leave and immediately turned and looked up at our house to see if I was standing there watching him. I hid so he couldn't see me but kept watching him. He stared at our house for a long time. He then dropped his head, put his hands in his pockets, and walked slowly toward the house.

When he opened the door, I was standing there, and it startled him. This time, I gave him a warning while pointing my finger at him. I warned him to stay away from his uncle before he got hurt. Hicks looked squarely in my face, and he pointed his finger back at me and into my face and said, "My uncle ain't going to hurt me, he is going to burn you up in this house while you are sleep." He didn't raise his voice and said it as if we were having a regular normal conversation. But unlike the time before, I knew Hicks meant what he said, and this time, I took the threat seriously. Although, I didn't immediately leave and move out my things, I was hardly ever there. I would go to my parent's house so that I could peacefully sleep. During the weekends, we would be off at the same time, and so I would go there with our daughter so we could spend some time together as a family. For some reason, I felt that I was safe if my daughter was there.

Hicks continued to change for the worse, and even our weekends together were spent arguing. I continued to fuss at him and warn him to tell his uncle to stay away from our house and told him that if he didn't watch himself that he too would be killed by him. Hicks would burst into laughter and say, "My uncle is going to kill you!" To make matters worse, he had even started to make our daughter repeat his words. Hicks would say, "Tell your momma that you wish she was dead." Our daughter would repeat what he told her to say, and he would laugh. I would listen to her sweet little angelic voice say, "I wish you were dead momma," then she would imitate his laugh. At the time, our daughter was two years old, only a few months from turning three. I knew she was too young to understand what her words meant, but it still hurt hearing them coming from her little voice. She sat in her dad's lap as she said them; thinking she and daddy were playing a funny game. I would fight back tears, and they burned in my throat. But I had learned early from childhood to never let those who hurt you see you cry.

With each confrontation, Hicks became increasingly distant, and withdrew himself even further from me. As soon as daylight came, he could be found outside under his car working on it, and I would be in the house unable to rest because he was constantly raising and lowering his car's engine. When I'd peep out at him, I noticed that he would always have his car propped up on the most raggedy carjack that he could find, and he would still crawl under it. He would drive me crazy revving the engine while underneath it. His car became his favorite girl, and most of his income was spent adding things to her to make her even more sporty and sharp. In fact, I had noticed he had begun to care more about his car than his own appearance. He had stopped combing his hair, and so his huge afro was usually filled with dirt and debris from lying on the ground underneath his car. He had even started to lose a lot of weight. I would fix him hearty meals but would watch as he tossed my food when he thought I wasn't looking. I believe someone had convinced him that he shouldn't trust me. Apparently, he listened because eventually he stopped eating anything that I prepared.

One Saturday morning, I heard Hicks outside revving up his car like he did every Saturday. I routinely got up and peeped out at him through the window. It was early in the morning, and it was hazy, so I could only see his legs sticking out from under the car. Suddenly, a shadowy figured creeped towards Hicks while he lay under the car. It was his uncle, and due to the haze, I never saw his car parked behind Hicks's car. As he got closer to Hicks and his car, I left the window and went to the front door which Hicks had left open, so I could get a closer view. His uncle positioned himself right near the car's jack and stood there watching Hicks; never saying a word. Hicks continued to rev the engine and wasn't even aware that he had a visitor standing there. I watched and wondered what his uncle's next move was going to be. When I saw him move closer to the carjack, I made a noise to let him know that I was standing there, and it startled him. Hicks's uncle quickly stepped back from the jack, and he tapped Hicks on his shoe with his shoe. He then called out his name, and Hicks quickly slid from under the car. Hicks looked spooked, and once he stood up, I saw him look back in the direction of his uncle's car that he never heard drive up. I could tell Hicks's uncle's visit surprised him. They spoke for a short moment and his uncle left. I believed the conversation was short because his uncle saw that I never moved from the door, and I continued to watch their interaction. As they spoke, Hicks's uncle's eyes quickly and constantly darted on and off me as I stood in the doorway. Soon he walked back to his car and drove away. Hicks turned off his car, and slowly walked to the porch. When he came into the house, I told him what I had seen, and gave him another verbal warning about his uncle, but this time he didn't say a word.

Days turned into weeks, and Hicks and I were still doing our same routine. After the last visit to Hicks on that hazy Saturday morning, Hicks's uncle never came to visit us again. He had finally gotten the message that I didn't want him there, and I believed he got it when I told Hicks during a heated argument that I was going to get a gun from my daddy, and if I saw his uncle at our house again, I was going to blow him away. It was nice not having him hovering around, but our peace from him was short lived. He had found a new way to interrupt our lives, and now he could contact Hicks without visiting. We did not have a home phone, but our neighbor did. Hicks's uncle would call our neighbor and have her tell Hicks that he was calling. She would come out on her porch, and yell over to us. She would yell to Hicks, "Your uncle said come to his house!" Hicks would jump in his car and leave, and he would not return for hours. He would never tell me what his uncle wanted or why he was going to his uncle's house so often.

One day, I wouldn't let him leave, and made him tell me

what was going on. His response hit me like a ton of bricks when he said, "My uncle has another wife, and he wants me down there to help her." I said, "Help her do what?" He told me that his new aunt had a niece, and his uncle was always calling him to come and pick her up or drop her off in Alexander City. I asked him, "Where in Alexander City?" Hicks would not tell me and wouldn't tell me anything more about the girl. I became angry and jealous of this mystery girl who required so much of my husband's time. I believed that this was a plot by his uncle to finally and completely break us up. One day, I finally got to see the mystery girl while I was at a local gas station. She drove into the gas station in one of Hicks's uncle's cars. I wasn't even aware she could drive since Hicks was always picking her up and dropping her off. I watched as she got out of the car and went in the store. She was very young, and distinctive looking. She had big brown eyes, long hair, and a slender build. I thought to myself how strange this girl looked, and wondered who Hicks's uncle was married to, and how the young girl fit in. After I left the store, I headed back to my parent's house. On the way there, I had to pass by Hicks's uncle's house. I noticed something very strange standing in his front yard. I slowed down to get a good look, and saw a small calf standing in his front yard tied to a tree. The calf looked sick and starved, and it was so small. I could see its ribs, and its hide was bruised and mangy looking; especially around its neck because it had large blotchy patches that almost resembled burns. When I got to my parent's house, I told them about the girl and the calf. My dad was there, and he told me that he had also seen the calf and wondered why he had not put the poor thing out of his misery. He also said he wasn't the only one who felt this way because he'd spoken to several of his friends and people in the community about the calf, and they all seemed to feel the same. He said everyone he talked to agreed that it was an eyesore and should have been put down because it looked so thin and frail.

We were in full conversation about the calf when one of my siblings that was still in high school entered the room. He had overheard our conversation about the girl. He told us the girl was his friend and that she was in his class. I told him how weird I thought she looked, and he told us that she was a little different but was very nice. He went on to say that one day while waving bye to her he saw strange symbols in her hand when she waved back at him. He said they looked as if they had been branded into her hand. When he asked her what they were, she quickly closed her hands, folded her arms, and got off the bus. For hours, we sat discussing the girl and her symbols, and tried to figure out what they could have meant. The discussions finally ended, so I got up and went home. On my way home, I couldn't shake the uncomfortable feelings I had towards Hicks's uncle, and his new wife's niece that I found out could drive, but always seemed to need a ride.

Hicks soon grew tired of the frequent calls. He began to get enraged when our neighbor called his name from her porch to tell him that his uncle wanted him. One day he said, "I am sick of picking her up!" I then said, "Then why don't you tell them that you are tired of picking that little gal up!" When he got up to leave, I asked him if I could go with him to pick her up, and he said, "There is no way that I can let you come." I asked him why not, and he responded that he just couldn't, and didn't give me an explanation and left. After he left, to keep myself busy until his return, I decided to do some dusting and topical cleaning. As I was cleaning, I noticed that all the items that had been given to us by Hicks's uncle had disappeared. When Hicks finally returned, I asked him where the items were. He told me his uncle had asked for them back. I was surprised when Hicks told me this, and I was shocked he had given them back without even telling me about it. Surely, he knew that I would eventually see that they were gone. This made me feel really scared, and I got an eerie feeling. I thought that maybe his uncle had taken the items back because he didn't want them to get burned up in the house; since supposedly that was his plan for me. Hicks and I got into an argument about it, but it was soon time for him to go to work, and so he left.

Later that night, my new ride to work came and picked me up, but I could barely focus. I thought about Hicks and his uncle and tried to piece together everything Hicks had told me. The next morning, when I got off from work, my ride dropped me off at the end of my driveway. Normally, my ride would take me up into my yard, but that morning she did not. As I started up our long driveway towards the house, I didn't see Hicks's car. I said to myself, "Where's Hicks and the baby?" Usually, when he got off from work, he would go to my parent's house or to his mom's and pick her up and bring her back home. But that morning he wasn't there, and it struck me as odd. As I got closer to my house, my mind told me not to go in. Something literally made me turn around. I walked back down the driveway and walked to the gas station up the road from my house. I waited at the gas station until someone I knew came by, and I then asked them if they could give me a ride to my parent's house. When I got to my parent's house, I had my brother drive me back home because I was too afraid to go alone. Before we left, I asked him to bring a gun. When we arrived at my house, I had my brother unlock the door and go through it to check it out. After his clearance, he waved at me in the car to come in. I went in and gathered my clothes and my daughter's clothes and left everything else. While I was gathering my things, my heart was pounding. I don't know why I was afraid, but I was. I was so nervous that I asked my brother to stand in my bedroom's doorway so he could protect me in case someone jumped out. My brother took my fear seriously and remained watchful and guarded as I packed. He knew that his big sister was afraid for a reason, and he was there willing to protect me if he had to. As I walked out of the door and on to the porch, I glanced back at our beautiful little cozy home, and then closed and locked the door. To this day, in my mind, I can still see the beautiful linoleum on the floors, and how neat and clean it was when I was leaving. I really loved my little house, but knew it was no longer safe for me to stay there.

Later that day, Hicks came to my parent's house with our daughter to pick me up. I questioned where he was and had been with our baby. In an arrogant and sarcastic voice, he said, "Why?" I said, "Because, I expect you and our baby to be there when I get off of work because I look forward to seeing her when I get home." Hicks totally ignored my statement and said, "Well, we spent the night at my mom's house." Then before I could ask another question, he immediately asked me if I was ready to go home. I replied, "I ain't never going back to that house again!" He stood there staring at me in disbelief. He then asked me if I would rather go back to his mom's house instead, and I yelled, "Hell no!" He tried to lower his voice; hoping that his lowered voice would convince me to lower mine. He didn't want my parents and siblings to hear our discussion. Then Hicks said, "Well, if you don't come home then I won't either." I don't know if he was trying to give me an ultimatum, but he then told me that if I didn't come back home, he was going to lock up the house and move back in with his family. I waved my hands, and then told him that I guess that's what he would have to do because I would not be going back. Some years later, I thought back to the conversation. It was revealed to me, that Hicks was just as afraid as I was to return to that house. I'll never know for sure if Hicks's words were real about his uncle's plan for me, but something had him afraid to return without me. Maybe, it was because I was foiling a well thought out plan and plot, and this would anger someone. I don't know, but I knew I felt safer at home with my family, so maybe Hicks did too.

Sometime later, after I wouldn't return to the house, Hicks allowed his sister and her husband to move in. When we left our house, everything was in place, so his sister and her husband were able to move right on in. When I saw Hicks's sister one day at the store, she told me that Hicks would often return to the house to visit her and her husband. She said that sometimes, he would even stop back to have dinner with them. Hicks had finally given up on asking me to come home. However, we were still meeting up to have companionship, and would go out on dates. We began to act more like we were dating instead of married, and I must admit, he was giving me more attention.

Hicks was still not himself, and when we were together, he'd seem melancholy. He started doing a lot of reminiscing about the past, and often talked about what he wished could be. He would discuss family members that he had not seen in a long time, and how he wished he could see them. One day, while listening to the O'Jays song "Family Reunion", he became sad and emotional. He talked about all his dead family members, and then said he wished that the ones still living would come together and have a big celebration. As I sat and listened to him going on and on about his family and a reunion, I too wished that there was a way to give him this reunion. This was the first time in a long time that I had seen him genuinely interested in something other than his car. We sat for hours talking, and eventually went in the house so he could play and visit with our daughter. After an hour or so, we said our goodbyes and he left.

The next morning, Hicks came and picked me up from work. He seemed to be in good spirits, and in a good mood unlike his melancholy behavior from the day before. We were traveling down Highway Twenty-Two, and connecting with Highway Nine, when we saw two people walking towards us. I asked Hicks if he knew who the people were, and he said that he didn't. He said that he'd never even seen them around before. As we were approaching them, I asked Hicks to slow down. I rolled down my window, so I could get a good closer look at them before we passed. When we got right up on the two individuals, I leaned out of the window to see them better. Hicks completely slowed down so that we could get a good look at them, but when I looked in to their faces, they didn't have one. I asked Hicks, "Did you see that?" He said, "What?" I said, "They didn't have a face!" Hicks responded, "They sure didn't." I tried to get him to turn around and go back but he wouldn't, I could tell that what he saw had creeped him out like it did me. I continued to try and figure out who the couple could have been. It was later revealed to me that maybe it was Hicks and I, "facing" what was to come. That day, I watched the couple in my passenger review mirror as we drove on down the road. I don't know why, but for some reason I thought that the couple would disappear. I felt this way since they didn't have faces, and I thought to myself that maybe they were ghosts. The couple never disappeared, but they continued to walk down the road; heading towards the cozy little house that Hicks and I once shared.

Hicks dropped me off and went on his way to wherever it was that he went. I went in and sat down and talked to my mom, but I didn't tell her about the couple that Hicks and I saw, but I was still on my mind. I had to go to work that night, so I went in my room and laid down to rest. I felt so at peace because I knew that my parent's home was safe, and they wouldn't allow anything to happen to me, so when I slept, I slept deep. Later that night, while I was sleeping; one of my baby sisters came in to my room and woke me up. She told me that I had a phone call. I got up and answered it, and it was Hicks's uncle's new wife. I was surprised by the call because I had never met her or spoken to her. However, there she was, on the phone requesting to see me. It was seven p.m., and since she knew my location, I'm sure someone had advised her that I worked the night shift, but she woke me up any way. When I said hello, Hicks's uncle's new wife asked me to come to her house. I was thrown off by her request because she had never invited me before, and she'd been married to Hicks's uncle for a while. I said, "Come to your house for what?" She responded by telling me that she had something to tell me. I asked her why she couldn't tell me over the phone. She responded, "I just can't, I need you to come up here." I told her, "I ain't coming up there, and I slammed down the phone, and told my sister not to wake me again until eight thirty p.m., when it was time for me to get up for work. When I went back to bed, I could hear the phone ringing again. I heard my little sister telling the caller that I went back to sleep, and that I wouldn't be taking any more calls because I had to go to work. Thinking back, I didn't give the call a second thought, and when my mom asked me about the call later, I was very nonchalant about it. My mom wasn't, and was very concerned, and I should have been as well.

My mom was off that week, so at nine fifteen; my naïve butt jumped in her car, and I went on to work that night without a care. In fact, I used her car and drove myself to work that entire week. My route to work was a pitch-black dirt road, with no houses for a long stretch. But, for some reason, I wasn't afraid. I knew and believed in God, and I knew that He would protect me because I had learned early that I was covered by His grace. Since I was a child, I had experienced many bad things early in my life, but God always kept me safe. I first fell in love with God when I was five years old. One morning, while playing and being fast on my grandmother's porch, my aunt who was two years older than me said, "You know you got to die one day?" I stopped dead in my tracks and thought about how care free and good I felt and didn't want it to end. Her statement scared me, but my aunt then comforted my fears by telling me how good God is, and that He watches over us and protects us. I then asked her where God was, and she told me that He was in heaven watching everyone; looking at the good and bad things they did. I told her I was going to be good from then on, so I could please the God that was in heaven. My aunt then taught me the Lord's Prayer, and when I would spend the night with her, we would recite it. My grandmother would wake us each morning with beautiful hymns that she sang to the Lord, and I often duplicated those songs each day when I missed the bus and had to walk to school. My worship service with God would cause me to be even later. Now, there I was in my twenties, traveling to work on that same dusty road from my child hood. Instead of the road having an early morning glow like it did when I walked to school, it was now pitch black. I guess the prayers and relationship with God from my youth is what kept me safe on that dusty road as I traveled it alone. Those same prayers also possibly kept me alive when death came for me a few days later.

The weekend rolled around again, and it was time for Hicks and me to have our date. It felt as if our relationship had started to get a little stronger. We were starting to bond since his uncle could no longer just pop up and lurk at our house or call the next-door neighbor's phone. We were now free to love each other without interference. Hicks now seemed to be o.k. with me not living with him, and I believe that he knew why I felt safer at my parents. Plus, he didn't have to worry about protecting me because he knew my mom and dad would. When Hicks picked me up for our weekend date, he decided to take me out to a club. He told me that his baby sister wanted to go and asked me if it was okay. I told him it was, so we drove to his mom's house and picked her up then headed for the club. We were riding and listening to music when I thought about the phone call I'd gotten from Hicks's uncle's wife. As Hicks drove, I looked over at him and said, "Oh by the way, your uncle's wife called me and woke me up out of my sound sleep the other night." He didn't say anything at first, but after an uncomfortable pause he asked, "What did she want?" I told him that she called and asked me to come to her house because she had something to tell me. I then asked him if he would take me over there before we went to the club, so that I could see what she wanted. His sister chimed in and said, "Yes, let's go up there." Hicks didn't respond and kept looking straight ahead. Hicks's sister and I started to insist that he take us there. He got defensive, and yelled, "I ain't gonna take you up there!" I asked, "Why not?" Hicks responded, "I ain't gonna let them kill my wife." I said, "So, is that what they want to do to me, kill me?" Hicks then said, "If yawl don't shut up about going up there, I'm gonna take both of you back home." Hicks never looked in my direction but kept his eyes straight ahead.

Hicks's, comments should have frightened and spoiled my night, but when you're young and have your youth, you believe that dying is for old people. I shook it off and continued to believe I had a full life ahead of me. I also believed that my husband loved me and would never let anything happen to me because we had reignited our love for each other, and we were best friends again, plus we had a daughter.

Sunday came, and we went to church as a family. After church, we got ice cream and rode around visiting family to show off our daughter. The weekend seemed like it zoomed by because we had so much fun. That Monday, I dreaded going back to work because now I would have to get a ride to work. But, like always when I got off, Hicks was there to pick me up. When I got into the car with him that morning, I snuggled up next to him, and we headed in the direction of my parent's house. When we turned off Highway Number Nine on to the dirt road a few miles down the road from my parents, Hicks slowed down because we had begun to kiss and caress each other. Hicks then stopped kissing me and said in anger, "What the hell does he want now!" I looked at him surprised and confused then said, "Who?" Hicks said, "My uncle!" I looked back to see a brown Lincoln Continental a short distance behind us. Hicks stopped the car and hesitated before he got out because he didn't want his uncle to see his erection. He was nervous and reached for the key to turn off the ignition, but I yelled, "Don't even think about it!" Hicks left the car running, and then got out. I moved into the driver's seat. I watched as Hicks stuck his hands in his pockets and dropped his head and walked back to his uncle's car. His uncle rolled down his window, and I watched as his uncle yelled at him. I could tell his uncle was upset because I could see his face and watched how his head bobbed back and forth. I could also tell that he was getting on to Hicks about something when I saw the look on Hicks face as he glanced back towards the car at me.

After the conversation was over, instead of coming down the road past me, his uncle backed his car completely back down the dirt road to the highway. Hicks quickly walked back to the car, and when he got there, I told him that I would drive. He then said, "No, I'll drive." I hesitated but slid back over into the passenger seat. When Hicks was in the car, I asked him what his uncle wanted, and why it was so important that he needed to follow us. He told me that his uncle needed him to come to his house as soon as he dropped me off but would not tell me why. I pressured him and he remained vague, so I left him alone. Hicks quickly took me home and left.

When I got to work that night, I went to my supervisor and asked for a transfer to the plant where Hicks and my mother worked. I told my supervisor that I really needed the transfer because I didn't have a car, and I would no longer be able to get to work. I told my supervisor that the transfer would place me at the same plant with my husband and mom. My supervisor was reluctant because he didn't want to lose me because I was one of his best spinners at the plant. I told him that my only other option would be to quit, and he felt sorry for me and gave me the transfer.

The next night, Hicks was off from work, so he was able to take me to work. When he picked me up it was about eight thirty p.m., and we headed out on our usual route through the dirt road that connected with Highway Number Nine. Once we got almost to Hicks's uncle's house, his car quit. Hicks tried repeatedly to make it start, but it wouldn't. However, he was able to put it in neutral and jump start the engine as it rolled down the hill. The engine continued to sputter, and wouldn't start, so he let the car coast down the hill, and it ended up in his uncle's driveway. He turned in and placed the car in park as my heart began to pound. Hicks turned to me and said, "We got to get my uncle to take you to work." I looked at him, and then looked back at the house. I sat there staring, and Hicks said, "You'll be okay." I searched for his eyes in the darkness to get reassurance but could only see the shadow of his afro. I thought to myself, "Well here it goes." Hicks got out of the car, walked around to my door, and opened it. I got out and he guided me towards the house, and up on the porch. He knocked on the door and his uncle soon opened it. Hicks immediately started to explain what had happened, and what we needed from him. Hicks told his uncle that I had to be at work at ten and needed him to take me. When Hicks said my name, his uncle stared directly at him, and never gave me a glance. I felt very awkward and uneasy standing there. Especially, at the door of the man who his nephew claimed wanted to burn me up while I slept, and at the door of a man who I felt was trying to destroy my marriage. I remained calm, but could hear my heart beating in my ears as I thought to myself, "Could this be a setup?" My wheels were turning because I found it strange how Hicks's car had stopped where it did. To me, it seemed very convenient, and at that moment I had the strongest desire to go home but knew I couldn't.

I then heard the voice of the man I loathed say, "Yawl come on in and sit down." Hicks held the door and motioned for me to go in, but I couldn't move. He saw that I wouldn't budge, so he went in first and I followed. The screen door slammed behind me, but I left the front door partially open. Hicks's, uncle told us to sit down, and motioned us toward his dinner table. He didn't have on shoes, so he disappeared in the back to get them. I was so scared. This was the first time I had ever been inside one of Hicks's uncle's houses, and that close to him. I looked around and saw a very un-kept house filled with junk and clutter. I wondered where his wife was, so I asked Hicks. He told me that she lived next door. The house next door was the house his uncle had shared with his first wife.

While sitting at the table, I noticed a lot of mail on it. I looked at it without touching it and saw that most of it had baby faces on it, and when I looked closer, they were Gerber Insurance policies. Hicks's uncle appeared back in the room, and said in a deep southern drawl, "Yawl ready to go?" Hicks leaped to his feet and so did I, and almost fell over backwards. Hicks caught me and guided me to the front door as his uncle followed us out. His uncle led us to one of the many cars that were parked in his front yard. When we reached the car, Hicks opened the back door behind his uncle for me to get in, and then he went around the back of the car to the other side and got in the back seat with me. He slid close to me and placed his arm around my shoulders. I snuggled close to him and forced a smiled; all the while searching his eyes for clues. He smiled back at me and hugged me tighter, and for some reason, I knew it was not my night to die.

I looked towards the front seat in the direction of his uncle and was wondering why he had not started the car. That's when he let out a loud demand, "Go move that car outta the way!" Hicks quickly jumped out of the car and ran over to his. He tried to start it, but it would sputter and jerk. He finally moved it, and he parked it slightly in his uncle's now third wife's yard. Hicks's, uncle started the engine and the panel lit up in green light. He turned around and glared at me in the back seat and said, "You can get up here in the front with me if you wanna." I looked at him with bugged eyes and a sneer of disgust, and said, "I don't wanna get up there with you!" Hicks's, uncle jerked back around as if we had never spoken, and never looked back again, not even into the rearview mirror.

I guess my anger overshadowed my fear because it had really pissed me off when I heard him yell at my husband in front of me. I knew he was his uncle, but there is a certain way a man should speak to another man in front of his wife. This was the first time that I had actually heard him speak to Hicks up close and personal because I had watched most of their interaction through windows, front doors, and rearview mirrors. Now, I had gotten to hear his actual tone, and I didn't like it one bit.

Hicks quickly walked back to the car, and got in to the backseat with me, and slid into his original position with his arm around my shoulders. That night, I got to work faster than Hicks had ever gotten me. I don't know if his uncle was uncomfortable because Hicks and I was sitting directly behind him, or because of the way I had spoken to him earlier without fear but anger. All I knew is that I didn't care for his uncle, and I believed he had done everything in his power to intimidate and scare Hicks into not being with me. When we arrived at my job, Hicks got out, walked around to my side, and opened the door and escorted me to the plant's door. He said, "I'll see you in the morning," and we exchanged a kiss and a hug and went our separate ways.

The next morning, Hicks was not there to pick me up. I thought maybe he had overslept. I waited around for a little bit, but after he didn't show, I caught a ride home from a co-worker.

Sooner or later I knew he would show up because he always did. When I got home, I did my routine and went to bed. When I woke up that evening, Hicks still had not shown up, and it was time for me to go to work again. My dad was home that night and said that I could drive his car to work, but instead I asked my brother to take me. I felt weird and uneasy since I had not heard from Hicks. We left the house a little early that night because I wanted my brother to drive me around our small community, so I could see if I could find Hicks's car. After about thirty minutes of looking, we stopped, so my brother could take me to work. The next day was Friday, and when I got off Hicks still was not there. I became really worried, but again caught a ride home with a co-worker. When I got there, I was expecting to see Hicks's car, but it wasn't there. I thanked my co-worker and ran into the house to see if Hicks had come by or called. My family said that he had not, and I sat puzzled and uneasy.

By six p.m., I was a nervous wreck because I still had not heard from Hicks. My mom and I both took that Friday night off from work, so we could go look for him. It was drizzling rain that day and overcast. I don't know what was worse, the cloudiness or my cloudy mind. My mom decided to drive because she knew that I couldn't focus. She tried to keep reassuring me that Hicks was okay, and that we would find him. We went to his mother's house first, and my mom stayed in the car while I ran in. Hicks's mom and his other family said that they had not seen him but didn't seem worried. This eased my mind a little so I sat down for a bit to ask if they knew where he might be. They gave me a couple of places to go and look and told me not to worry. While sitting there, Hicks's mom asked me, "Have you seen the white car?" I said, "White car, what white car?" The family became quiet and looked at each other. I asked about the white car again and was told by his mom and family that a white car had been following several of them to work and around town. I then asked, "Could you see who was in it?" They told me no and said that they had never seen it in the community before. I found this very strange, and I wondered why it was following Hicks's family members around.

I told the family that my mom was in the car and I had to go. They told me that they believed that Hicks was okay, and to tell him to come home and check in when I saw him and said that they would do the same if he came home first. I told them I would, and I left. When I got in the car, I told my mom about what Hicks's mom and the family had asked me about the white car. She also said that it seemed strange that someone would be following them, and then told me that I would need to be careful because there was no telling what was going on. My mom and I then drove from one Hicks's friend house to another, but still could not find him. We went to the last friend's house that I knew of, but no one was there. As we were leaving the driveway of that friend's house, and heading back down their narrow driveway, and up a hilly road; we met Hicks's car driving erratically, and it almost hit us head on. Hicks's car was speeding and driving in the middle of the road, and if my mom had not swerved there would have been a terrible collision. He never stopped, never slowed down, and there was no way that my mom could have turned around to follow it or even catch up to it. The car disappeared over one of the hills and was gone from view. This seemed so strange because Hicks knew my mom's car, and I wondered why he didn't stop when he saw us or when it almost hit us. We were very shaken up by the almost collision, so we decided to go back home, and gave up on trying to connect with him.

Hicks had been gone for two nights, and that second night was the longest night of my life. I tossed and turned in my bed, and my mind tried to figure out where Hicks was going when we saw his car earlier that day because he was supposed to have been at work. The next day was Saturday, and I thought to myself, "Surely Hicks will come today." He had never stayed away this long since we married, and it was going on day three. I was so worried and all I could do was sit around the house and wait. Gloom had set in on me. I started trying to piece together possible clues, and I searched my brain for information he had told me in conversations, so I could find his possible location. At about six p.m. the phone rang, and I answered it. When I said hello, it was Hicks, and he was hysterically screaming my name over and over again. All I could say was, "Hicks, where are you?" I begged and pleaded for him to tell me, but all he could say, and repeat was my name, and he sounded desperate. The next voice I heard was the operator saying, "I'm sorry sir, but your three minutes are up," and the phone disconnected. Once the call had ended, I waited and waited for him to call back. I stayed near the phone for what seemed like forever; even after my eyes grew heavy from exhaustion. The next morning, I woke up achy and stiff; still sitting in the chair next to the phone.

Around twelve thirty p.m. that Sunday afternoon, I heard Hicks's car coming up the road, and my heart sank. I didn't know what to expect, so I walked out on the porch, and watched as his car came into the yard. I watched as the door to his car opened, and he got out of it, and walked up to the porch. Hicks looked like a corpse. He was so very pale and thin, and his eyes were bloodshot red. His hair was matted to his head and his clothes were wrinkled and dirty. He looked as if he had not had a bath for all the days that he had been gone. Our eyes met as he got closer to the porch, but he could not hold eye contact with me. I asked him where he had been, and why didn't he talk to me on the phone when he called. All he could do was shrug his shoulders and shake his head, and he wouldn't give an answer. I tried and tried to pry the information out of him, and when he wouldn't tell me I got angry. I shoved and pushed him and tried to make him react. I soon gave up when I stared into his face and saw that he didn't even have the energy to fight back. I saw a man feeble and childlike when I looked at him, so I grabbed him and pulled him to me, and tightly hugged him. As I held him in my arms, I could feel his thin and fragile body within my embrace. I could tell that he wanted to melt in my arms, but also knew it would come with more questions if he did, so he quickly hugged me back and then released me.

Hicks fought my stares of concern and continued to hold on to the secrets from his three-day disappearing act. He had practically just come to show me that he was alive because he didn't even stay five minutes. He told me he had to go because he had not seen his mom, and he said that he would see me again on Monday morning when he picked me up from work. I interrupted his attempt to leave, and I told him that our daughter had been asking about him and looking for him. I tried to make him go in to see her and stay because we had not seen him for three days. He didn't respond, and the more I tried to talk to him, the more he continued to walk towards his car; acting like he didn't hear me. Hicks got in his car and sunk behind the wheel, and hesitated before he fired up his engine. As he backed out of the driveway, he kept his eyes focused on me instead of looking behind him as he maneuvered the car. When the car was facing the road, he looked back at me once more, then drove away.

I went in the house and tried to piece together our five minute or less visit. My mom and siblings questioned me when I came through the door and didn't see him in tow. I had no explanation for them because he had not given me one. I could tell from my mom's squinting eyes, she was suspicious about his whereabouts, and I knew she thought that maybe he was with another woman because usually that's where my dad was. I let her continue in her suspicions because she didn't see what I had just saw, and that was Hicks looking as if he had just come back from the brink of death. I went in my room, and laid across the bed, and cried; pondering what could be going on with my young husband, and questioning why he wouldn't let me in.

That Monday, Hicks picked me up just like he said he would, and when he did; he acted as if nothing had happened that weekend. As we headed towards my parent's house, I wanted to bring it up, but didn't want to make waves, and so I didn't. I was still worried though because he still looked so tired and stressed. I believed that he could feel my anxiety, so he leaned over and kissed me. I then reached over and kissed him back and hugged him. We were civil all the way down the road and continued to exchange kisses and hugs. I believe we both were truly happy to see each other; after all, we were young lovers who just so happened to be married. Plus, I had just undergone two nights and 3 days without seeing my best friend and love of my life, so I was just glad to be in his presence again.

We turned off the highway and headed towards my parent's house. However, before we reached the house, we decided to veer off to one of our favorite places in the woods to grab a little quality time alone. We often went there to talk, make love, and just enjoy nature. Once Hicks turned into the trail, I don't know why, but I felt like maybe it wasn't such a good idea. I felt uneasy because Hicks's uncle always seemed to pop up. He seemed to do it every time we tried to be alone, and the trail we were entering was narrow. I knew that I didn't want to get stuck or blocked in facing the wrong direction. Plus, I still had not forgotten about Hicks's unexplained three-day disappearing act, and his panicky call to me the night before his return. However, I still trusted Hicks, and wanted to believe that he was going to tell me everything, and that he would possibly do it after our little private session in the woods.

Once Hicks entered the trail, something told me to look back. When I did, I saw a car slowly turning in behind us. The car was white in color, and immediately I knew that this was the car that Hicks's family had told me about the day before. I realized and knew that my life was at stake. I didn't know if it was a setup by Hicks, or if the car had been following us the whole time, and we just didn't see it because we were too into each other to notice. Looking at the car easing its way up behind us, my mind told me that it was there for me, and I knew for sure that I was going to die that morning, if the person or persons in the car got a hold of me. I started screaming and pleading, "Hicks, don't let them get me!" Please, please don't let me see who is in that car!" Hicks looked back, and then looked at me. His eyes darted from me to his review mirror, and then back at me again with fear. He then yelled, "There's nothing I can do because I can't turn around!" He then said, "There are too many big rocks and trees in the way." I scanned his face for deceit, but I could tell from his face that he was literally in a panic. I kept screaming his name while begging him to get me out of there. While in the narrow trail, my eyes hopefully and skillfully searched our surroundings looking for a way out. I tried to calm myself, but I could hear my pulse beating in my ears. I held my breath and tried to calm my heart down long enough to think and see a way out. Although the car we were in belonged to Hicks, that morning I told him how to drive it. I instructed him where to turn the car around, and he followed my instructions to a tee. I can't remember all the instructions that I gave him, but after he completed my final step, we were facing the white car head-on. The white car had been inching down the narrow path towards us, but now it had come to a complete stop, and seemed to be waiting on us for its next move.

I looked over at Hicks and said, "I am ready to die, are you ready to die with me?" Hicks looked back at me with teary eyes, and said, "Yes." I then said to him, "What about our daughter?" He looked at me with sad eyes while shrugging his shoulders and said, "I don't know." I turned from his gaze and looked back at the white car that had started inching its way in to the trail again towards us. I placed my hands on the dash board and braced myself; preparing for impact. I took a deep breath, and then began spitting out driving commands to Hicks. I told him to put the car in first and quickly let up off the clutch and shift it to second and mash it. When he did as I instructed, the car took off like a rocket and began to fishtail. He wrestled to control the wheel, but when he got control, he floored the gas pedal, and headed straight towards the car. As we got closer to the white car, I could see that there were four black men inside of it, and I didn't recognize any of them.

The driver of the car soon realized that we were heading right for them. He quickly put their car in reverse and started backing up out of the trail, and he was driving just as fast backwards as we were driving forward. When they got to the end of the trail they swung to the right, and we went to the left. We never broke our speed, and the car seemed to get even faster as we headed towards my parent's house. Hicks was at full speed when I looked back to see if the car was following, but I could only see clouds of dust swirling behind us. The car soon came in view and tried to overtake us, but the dust became too thick for them, so they had to fall back, and I watched as they turned off onto an abandoned road. We continued to sail on up the dirt road, never reducing speed as the car tires rocked and roared over dirt and rocks and spat it back into the atmosphere.

When we had finally reached my parent's driveway, Hicks skidded into their yard, and was still going so fast that he almost hit the porch. When the car finally stopped, it jilted us forward, and we sat there frightened and exhausted. I asked him who were the people, and why were they chasing us, and he said he didn't know. I then asked how they knew about our spot, and he said that they must have followed us, but said again that he didn't know why they were following us. We had barely escaped, and we both knew that as we sat there trying to collect our thoughts about what had just happened. Hicks then startled me when he opened the door, leaned out of it, and began throwing up. I watched as he discharged green bile from his mouth, and it eventually turned into dry heaves. While he was leaning out of his driver's side door, I could see green spider webbed veins under his skin, and on his neck, were lesions that looked like bruises or burns. I then said, "Hicks, what is all that on your neck?" When I saw it, it reminded me of the blotches that I had once seen on the sickly calf tied to a tree in his uncle's yard. My question quickly made Hicks lean back in and close his car door. He sat back, rested his head on the headrest, and started pulling up his collar around his neck in an attempt to hide his scars. I grabbed his collar and tried to pull open his shirt, and he fought back in resistance trying to prevent me from seeing his neck. I got a good hold of his shirt and ripped it open, and it fully exposed his chest that looked as if it had been mutilated by something hard punching it, and small circular burns that resembled cigarette burns. Knowing that I had seen his scars, Hicks called my name in a child-like voice, and then said, "I'm sick." I felt so sorry for him. Hicks actually looked sick and weak by the eyes. However, I knew that he was trying to avoid my questioning, and I needed to know what had happened, and where the bruises came from. I questioned and questioned him, but he would just repeat that he was sick. While sitting there staring at him, I wondered how I hadn't noticed that morning when he picked me up from work how sick he looked. I guess I was just so glad to see him that I overlooked the obvious. I felt so helpless sitting there with him. I suggested to him that I would go in the house, get my brother, a gun, and then we'd take him to the hospital, so we could see what was wrong with him. Seeing my husband like this, I no longer gave a thought to the chase we had just endured, I just wanted Hicks to get well.

Hicks stared at me as I gave him my suggestions, and then he shook his head and sadly said, "No that's o.k." I then said, "Hicks, the doctor will know what's wrong with you, and will help you get better, let's go now!" He looked at me with no hope in his eyes and said, "The doctor can't help me." I said, "How do you know that the doctor can't, let's just go and find out!" Hicks dropped his head then told me, "I got to go now." I continued begging him not to leave, and to come into the house to give the people that chased us time to go away. He would not listen, and again told me that he had to go. I told him to at least come in and see his daughter before he left, and he told me, "I can't, I got to go." I got out of the car and walked up on the porch and shook my head at Hicks in disappointment as I looked at him. I watched as he backed out of the driveway looking the same way he'd looked the day before on that Sunday; again, staring intently at me as he backed out of the driveway.

I continued to stand on the porch as Hicks left. When he left the driveway, and entered back on to the dirt road, he headed in the opposite direction of the people that had chased us. He drove up the road erratically, and the car vanished into the dust that swirled around it, and to me it looked like a magic trick that had just ended in a puff of smoke. When the car and swirling dust disappeared over a hill and I could no longer see it, I could still hear the engine and gears being shifted by Hicks. I could even hear him when he got on the highway and traveled up Highway Number Nine.

Hicks would constantly work on and alter his cars, so they could make the sound that they did. He added dual mufflers and certain tires that would enhance the speed, and he did it to make sure that his car stood out from everyone else's in our community. I've been places with my mom when I heard someone say, "Here comes Hicks." A few minutes later, his car would either turn in or pass by. The sound from his car would get there before he did, and people admired his cars and his skill at altering them. On one of his cars, he had outside speakers on it, and he would play the latest music. Everyone knew he was a car lover and knew he liked to drive them fast, so it was no surprise when I could still hear his car several minutes after he had left.

I continued to stand on the porch to see how long I could hear the car, and the sound was starting to fade. I was about to go in to the house when I heard another car coming from the opposite direction. I stopped in my tracks and waited for it to appear. When I caught a slight view of the car, I saw that it was a white car, so I waited to see the model. The car climbed one hill and quickly disappeared under another. I stood frozen waiting for it to come fully in to view. Once it got closer, I saw it was the same white car that had followed and chased Hicks and me. I ran in the house hysterically and rambled out what was happening. My mom kept screaming, "What!" I must have looked like a bumbling fool to her, but I was finally able to get it out of my mouth that someone had tried to run us down, and they were on their way up the road.

My mom jumped up from where she was sitting and grabbed a Winchester shotgun from the gun rack over her bed, and I grabbed a twenty-two rifle. We both tore out of the house and stood on the porch with our guns drawn waiting for the car. The car was just about to turn into the driveway when the occupants saw us armed and ready for them. The car didn't completely stop but slowed to a crawl. It was as the occupants were contemplating whether they should turn on in anyways. It was almost as if they were daring us to open fire on them. I tried to get my mom to let us go ahead and shoot them, but she responded, "No, just wait, and let they asses come in here if they bad!" The white car and its occupants wisely turned from the driveways edge and cruised on by, but they took their sweet time; possibly watching us to see if we were going to move from our positions. We didn't move, and we watched them until they were completely out of sight.

My mom and I did not relax for the rest of the afternoon, even though she and I had to be at work later that night. When time came for us to go to work, we got ready and took our guns. My mom always stayed armed, and in addition to her pistol she carried a razor. My dad came home before we left, and we told him what had happened. He went into one of his dresser drawers and pulled out a thirty-eight pistol and gave it to me. It was as if this pistol was just for me. It had a pearl handle and was beautiful. My dad then told me not to be afraid to use it if I had to; especially if someone tried to stop us on our way to work. He told me to shoot first and ask questions later, and that's what I planned to do.

When we left for work, we headed in the same direction that Hicks and the white car had gone earlier. I went that way to see if Hicks's car was at his uncle's house because if it was, it would mean that he had missed work that day. As we passed, I didn't see it, and I felt relieved. When we got to work, to my surprise Hicks's car was there. My mom and I parked her car, and we began walking towards the plant. As we neared the plant, we had to pass by Hicks's car, and it looked as if it had been freshly washed and waxed. It was a full moon that night, and the car gleamed under it. It was almost like a spotlight, but the moonlight only highlighted the two front seats. The back of the car was dark, and it was as if the moonlight had cut the car in half and refused to shine on the back half of the car. I found it strange how the front was so bright, but a dark shadow hovered over the back half. My stare was broken when my mom said, "Oh, look at how Hicks's car is shining!" I walked up to the car and reached for the door handle but couldn't bring myself to touch it. I wanted to look in the backseat, but my mind wouldn't let me. It was almost like a force was holding me back from touching the car and peering into it. *I did not, and because of this, I often find myself wondering what might have happened if I had, and if it could have changed Hicks's life's course.* I stepped away from the car, and walked back towards my mom, and we went on into the plant.

We were a little late that night, and Hicks was getting ready to get off, and if we had been any later, we would have missed seeing him. When we entered the building, my mom went on to her job, and I went to mine. As I was getting ready to start up my machines, I saw Hicks walking my way, and he was walking fast. Without even a hello, Hicks walked straight up to me and said, "We should have another baby because I don't want our daughter to grow up alone without a sister or a brother." I found his statement odd, but answered, "Well, we can't have one right now." We were standing in the middle of the plant, and he looked as if he meant right at that moment. I hoped my response would get a smile or a chuckle, but after my statement, he stood there staring at me. I broke the silence by asking him where he'd gone earlier that day after he left me standing on the porch. He told me that he went home because he had to get ready for work. I then asked him, "Where are you about to go since you're off?" He said, "I'm going home." Then he asked me, "Where's the baby?" I said, "You know where she is, she is down to my parent's, and you need to go home, and please don't go down there messing with her because she's asleep." Hicks then said, "But, I want to see her because I didn't get to see her today or yesterday." I told him how that wasn't a good idea and told him again to leave our daughter where she was, and that he could see her the next day. His face seemed blank at my instructions, so I reaffirmed again, "Don't go trying to get her, and I mean it!" He stared at me as if he was looking through me, but responded, "I won't." I couldn't fathom why he would even ask knowing the dangers that we had experienced earlier that morning.

Hicks seemed to be rushing our conversation, and he continued to seem anxious to leave, so I tried to get out as many words as I could. I wanted to discuss the car chase by the goons earlier that morning, and wondered why Hicks had not brought it up, and seemed nonchalant about it. He acted as if it was a regular day; nonchalant enough to even pick up our daughter. He bounced from one leg to the other, as if he was waiting for me to shut up so he could leave, but purposely I started another conversation to hold him there. Hicks tried to leave again, but I stopped him and asked him if he would hang around for a while and talk to me because we had not spent enough time with each other. *Especially, since he went missing for three days, returned, and then we were chased by goons the next day.* He was about to tell me again that he had to go, but I interrupted him and asked him to help me set up my job for the night. I attempted to stall him by saying that I needed his help putting up my spools to start my textile threads. He looked blankly at me, and said, "I can't, I got to go." I then asked him where he was going, and he said that he was going to his mom's house. I asked him if he was sure that was where he was going, and he responded by saying, "It's Friday the thirteenth, I ain't going nowhere else." He then told me that he'd be there the next morning to pick me up. He gave me a long hug and a quick kiss and headed for the door.

Thinking back, if I had known that night would be the last time, I'd see him alive, I would have forced a longer conversation, or would have gotten my mom's help in making him stay longer. I wish I would have walked with him to his car, or even to the door so maybe I could have seen something, or someone as he opened the door to drive away. Instead, I wagged my head at him in disappointment, as he left me standing on the plant's floor. I stood there watching until his thin frame disappeared behind the slowly closing doors of the plant. As I stood there, I thought to myself, "Something is seriously wrong with Hicks because he will no longer listen to me or anyone." His mother even told me on several occasions, that he had stopped listening to her. She told me that his head had gotten hard, so she was going to stop trying to get some sense into it. Even though he seemed unreachable, I still believed that he was a good man, and that he loved me. But, as I watched those plant doors close completely behind him, I knew that I had lost the man that he once was, but I hoped that it wasn't for good.

Shortly after Hicks left, I started work. I worked as a spinner for the local textile mill and was responsible for maintaining a machine that turned thread into yarn. Once the yarn was completed, I would remove it and stack it on racks so it could be shipped. If the machine ran out of thread, it would halt production, and it was hell reloading the spools. I constantly walked each frame to make sure they didn't run out, and I made sure that they were running properly.

That night, one frame ran out before I could get to it. It was in the very back of the plant away from everyone and near a wall. As I neared the wall and machine, I began to hear loud voices behind me, so I quickly turned around to see who they belonged to, but no one was there. I stood there waiting to see if the people would appear or if the voices would start up again, but they didn't. Since no one appeared, I turned again and began to head towards the wall where the machine was waiting. I was almost to the wall when I got an eerie feeling, but I kept walking. When I got completely to the wall, I heard someone scream "Hey, Mary Dean!" in a blood curdling way. I quickly turned around expecting to see a person standing right behind me, but again no one was there. I stood there with my heart pounding and dumbfounded; not knowing what to do. I was scared. Not only was my heart beating fast, but my body started trembling. I remained still and tried to calm and collect my thoughts. My eyes quickly scanned my surroundings, and when I saw nothing, I forced myself to go on past the wall to the machine. My goal was to quickly rethread the new spool and get out of the isolated area. When I got to the frame, I started tying off the spools, and I was almost at the end of the frame when I heard a rush of different voices that hit me all at once. I couldn't make out nor understand what the voices were saying, but I heard voices of men, women, and children speaking with different pitches, and with different feelings. I could no longer contain my heart, and I almost fainted. I bolted from the machine and ran to find my mom. When I found her, I was in a panic and had tears streaming down my face. When she saw me, she said, "What in the world is wrong with you?" I said, "Momma, I hear a lot of voices talking, but I am not seeing anyone when I turn to face those voices." She stared at me in confusion, and then told me to calm down. I tried, but more words rambled from my mouth. My mom stared at me as if she was seeing someone she had never seen before. She yelled my name to make me stop rambling, and it snapped me back to reality. I went silent, and just stared at her through teary eyes. I knew that I must have sounded crazy to her, but I gathered myself enough to ask if she'd help me with my machine. I didn't want to be by myself. My mom said, "Okay, but give me a minute." I didn't move but stayed right there and helped her with her machine to help speed things along. When we were finished with her machine, we went to mine. It was completely down, so my mom suggested we take a break before we brought it back up. She shut off my machine, and we headed to the break area.

When we got to the breakroom, and right before we entered, I heard that single desperate voice yells out again, "Hey, Mary Dean!" The voice sent chills all over my body, but this time it seemed to drain all my strength, and I felt like a limp noodle. I quickly took a seat at a table, and my mom walked over to another table, and began talking to one of her coworkers. My mom glanced back over at me as she was talking, and when she saw my face, she quickly left her coworker standing there, and hurried back over to me. She said, "Dean, what's wrong!" I looked at her with tears rolling down my face and said, "Momma, I'm fixing to die because someone keeps calling my name, and I am hearing other voices." My mom quickly sat down and was silently staring at me while I cried.

This was not the first time that I had expressed concerns about my health to my mom. Weeks prior, I had noticed that my skin had started to darken, and I was also losing my hair. One day, my mom saw me holding my hands out in front of me examining them, and she asked what I was looking at. I then showed her my hands and asked if she saw how dark they were and how dark my skin was becoming. Before she could answer, I gave a slight tug on my hair, and showed her how easily it came out of my scalp. I could tell that it scared her, but she tried to hide her reaction. Not wanting to upset me further, she told me that I was overreacting and that I was going to be all right, but I saw concern in her eyes.

My mom broke her silence and told me to stop crying. She tried to reassure me again that I was okay and would be all right. After she said this, my tears began to fade. My mom stood up and said we should head back, so she could help me fix my machine. We walked back to the area I had fled from, and she helped me fix and reload my spools. As we left the area, and walked back to my other frames, she told me to come and get her if they went down again so I wouldn't be alone. Then my mom left me and went back to her job. That night, my production was very low because I spent most of my time in the company's restroom thinking about my situation. While I was in there, I didn't hear any voices, but I was still afraid. However, I felt much better since I had confided in my mom. Her words had given me some reassurance that I would be alright, and they stuck with me. I didn't hear the voices anymore that night, but I still thought about them. Every time they would try to creep back in, I fought them off by thinking about good things, and that helped me get through the night.

The next morning when I got off from work, I walked outside the plant and waited for my mom who was also getting off. When I got outside, I noticed that my mom's car was gone. When my mom came out of the plant, she told me that my brother had asked to borrow it while she was at work. He was supposed to come back and pick her up, but since he wasn't there, she didn't worry because she knew that she could catch a ride with me and Hicks. We both got off at six a.m., and Hicks was usually there waiting when I got off. This particular morning, he was late. After an hour, Hicks had not showed up, and I thought maybe that he had overslept, so we continued to wait. We watched as coworker after coworker started to leave the plant but didn't notice or realize that we didn't see anyone coming to work for the morning shift. Hicks still had not arrived, and I began to get very worried. I knew what happened the last time he didn't pick me up on time, and I didn't see him for several days. We were still waiting, and it was now ten a.m. and the plant had completely shut down. It was rare seeing the plant closure because it only shut down during the holidays; never in February, and never on the weekend.

I still wanted to wait for Hicks because I didn't want him coming all that way for me, and me not to be there waiting for him. The plant's parking lot became completely empty, and I told my mom I was worried. She said, "Girl, he'll be here, let's go sit down." We went and sat down and smoked our cigarettes and talked to pass time. After another thirty minutes passed, we knew that we would have to hitch a ride home. My mom and I walked to the main highway and waited until someone we knew came by and caught a ride home. The driver was a family member, but he charged us fifteen dollars for the ride. He said he was charging so much because our dirt road would get his car dusty. He lived less than two miles from us, and it was highway robbery, but we needed a ride home. To this day, I will never forget how we were treated in our time of need by this person, who was supposed to be blood.

When we got home, my mom's car was in the yard, and my brother was in the house fast asleep from his partying the night before. Normally, we got home about six thirty a.m., and would go in and go to sleep. Since we had been up for hours waiting on a ride, we were now restless. It was about twelve p.m. and it was a beautiful sunny day in February, so we did not want to go to bed. Instead, we went in the house to check on things, and then left to go look for Hicks. We decided to head to Hicks's mom's house first, and we took a shortcut to get there. On our way through the shortcut, we stopped at Hicks's mom's cousin's house. She had a son that looked like Hicks, and they could have passed for brothers, if people didn't know they were cousins because they looked so much alike. We decided to stop because we saw his van parked in his mom's yard, and I knew that he and Hicks often hung out. We parked on the side of the road in front of the house, and my mom honked the horn. The cousin came out of the house and walked towards our car. Before he could reach the car, I rolled down my window and yelled out to him and asked if he had seen Hicks. He then said, "Nah, I ain't seen

Hicks, give me a light?" By this time, he had fully made his way to our car. He bent down near my window, and he looked past me as if I wasn't sitting there, and then peered over to see who was in the driver's seat. He had an unlit cigarette in his hand, and asked again if he could get a light, but kept his eyes on my mom as if he was asking her. My mom didn't respond, so I picked up her lighter and handed it to him. Never exchanging a glance at me, he took the lighter from my hand and began to light his cigarette. I asked him again, "Have you seen Hicks?" When he lit his cigarette with trembling hands, and acted nervous from my question, I knew then that he had. This time he didn't answer and quickly dropped the lighter in his pocket and proceeded to walk away from us. My mom then said in a stern mean voice, "Give me back my lighter!" He partially turned around, and handed it to me without looking at us, and I snatched it from his hand as hard as I could. After I snatched the lighter from him, he didn't ask why I did it nor did he even glance in our direction, but quickly walked back across the yard and into his mother's house. I looked over at my mom and she looked back at me and said, "That Nigga's lying!" Then I said, "I know he is." My mom put the car in drive, and as she drove away, we continued to discuss Hicks's cousin's behavior as we headed to Hicks mother's house. We talked about how nervous he was, and how shifty his eyes were when he couldn't hold eye contact. We even discussed how shaky his hands were while trying to light his cigarette after my question, but most of all, how unconcerned he seemed. He didn't even offer to tell us that he'd let Hicks know that we were looking for him, if he saw or ran into him. At the time, my gut told me he didn't offer because he already knew where Hicks was.

I had never liked Hicks's cousin because I had gone to school with him; even then he was hardheaded and bad. As an adult, he wasn't any different, and I had heard talk about how he would do anything for money. It was rumored in the community that he too was somehow involved in the murders that was taken place. I believed the rumors because for a man that didn't have a job, he had been seen flashing large sums of money around town. He had also purchased a brand-new van and mobile home. However, he was not the only young man in the community without a job but was purchasing new things. Hicks had several male friends that he would periodically hang around, but suddenly he and his cousin had become very close buddies. I believe it was because Hicks was drawn to his cousin's newfound riches, and his shiny new van. I found out about their close new relationship one Saturday, when Hicks left the house and stayed gone for a long time. When he returned, I asked him where he'd been for so long. He told me that he had been up to his cousin's house hanging out and listening to music while riding around in his new van. I then asked Hicks, how could his cousin buy a new van when he didn't have a job. Hicks stood there looking blankly at me as if he had never thought about it. I then pointed and wagged my finger at Hicks and warned him that he better not get involve with his cousin and told him that he needed to stay away from him. I also warned him that if he didn't stay away, his cousin and uncle would be his downfall if he didn't watch out. He walked away from me that day and said, "I don't believe that!" I yelled at him as he was walking away, and told him to keep on not believing me, but one day he was going to wish that he had.

We turned into the driveway of Hicks's mom's house, and we drove slowly up the rocky driveway. When we got close to the house, my mom parked and turned off the car's engine. I looked over at her, and she told me to go ahead and go in, and she would wait in the car. I got out and walked up to the house. I walked up on the porch and peeped in through the screen door. Hicks's baby sister who we had taken with us to the club was in the living room watching television. I said hello through the screen, and she told me to come on in. When I entered, I immediately asked her if she had seen her brother. She started laughing, and in a playful manner said, "You done lost your husband, and mom done lost her son." I stared at her but felt some relief because I thought that since she was being comical; she had seen him and was teasing me about losing him. His sister then called out to their mom who was at the back of the house and announced that I was there to see her. When Hicks mother came into the living room, she was in tears. I quickly asked what was wrong. Through tears she said that she was worried about Hicks because she had not heard from him since the day before. I told her that I had seen him at work, and he told me that he was heading to her house. She then asked me if he had picked up our daughter. I told her that he hadn't but had wanted to. By this time, his mom was fully sobbing as if she knew something had happened to him, and that he wouldn't be coming home. Now, I was worried. I started to question her about any other places she thought he could be. Through her weeping, she said that she didn't know, but said she was really worried about Hicks and scared. His baby sister watched as we exchanged concerns, and she started making suggestions of where she thought he could be, but really couldn't offer any new information. I told them that I would keep looking, and that my next stop would be at his other sister's house; the oldest of Hicks three sisters. I walked out of the house and on the porch letting the screen door slam behind me. Normally, I would have held the screen door and eased it closed, but at the time I was too distracted by Hicks's mom's breakdown to even care. I walked across the yard and back to my mom's car. I saw her searching my eyes for information before I got there, but when I got in the car and closed the door, she automatically fired up the engine and asked where we should look next.

When we got to Hicks's sister's house, she came to the door before we had a chance to knock. I said hello to her and then asked her if she'd seen her brother. Immediately, she started screaming to the top of her voice. Not only did her uncontrollable screams scare me almost to death, but they brought her husband to the door in a panic. When her husband appeared, he asked what was wrong, but I didn't say anything because I was too focused on Hicks's sister and her reaction to answer him. I told Hicks's sister to calm down because I was only there to ask if she had seen her brother. His sister then put her hand over her heart, and said, "Oh, I thought that you were coming to tell me some bad news." I said, "No, I just wanted to know if you had seen your brother today?" She let out a big sigh of relief and said that she had not seen him that day. She then tried to remember the last time she had, and then said that she had not seen him for a while. She then reassured me that he would turn up soon. She said, "He'll show up, you know how my brother is." I said o.k., and we said our goodbyes.

My mom and I left and headed up the road to his other sister's house that was living in the house that Hicks and I once shared. When we got there, we saw that the car was gone but the door to the house was open. My mom honked the horn and Hicks's brother-in-law came out and headed towards the car. I got out of the car and joined him in the middle of the front yard. I asked him if he had seen Hicks, and he told me that he had not.

He also told me that it had been a while since he had seen him. I told him that I had a bad feeling that something had happened to him because no one seemed to know where he was, and I had not seen him since that Friday night at work, and that he was supposed to have picked me up from work but didn't show up. I also told him which family members I had already gone to see, but they had not seen or heard from him either. His brother-in-law dropped his head and wagged it from side to side. He then lifted his head and looked me in my eyes and said, "Something real scary just happened to me right before you pulled up and honked the horn." I stared at him because I was too afraid to ask what it was. He started to talk then paused while looking at me intently as if I wasn't going to believe him. He then told me that he was in the house listening to music, when all a sudden the radio station turned into static. He said that he went to the dials trying to get the station back when a loud voice came through the radio's speakers. He said that the voice screamed his name, and then told him to turn the radio down. He said it scared him, so he quickly turned down the radio, and was startled again by our car's horn. After he told me this, chills went all over my body and I could feel the hairs rising on the back of my neck. I believed him, and we discussed how we both felt that something bad had happened, or it was about to happen. I told him that I had to go but planned to keep looking for Hicks. He asked me where I was going next, and I told him to the local gas station, so I could see if someone had seen Hicks or his car. He told me that when Hicks's sister got back with the car, he would go and ask around too. He said that if he heard anything or saw Hicks, he would let me know or tell Hicks that I was looking for him. We gave each other a hug, and I walked back to the car where my mom was patiently waiting. I told her what was said, and although she didn't say much, I could tell that she had already begun to worry.

When we pulled into the gas station there was hardly anyone there. The gas station attendant was outside, so my mom drove over to him. When I rolled down my window, he leaned down into the car and said hello. We said hello and told him that we were looking for Hicks and asked if he had seen him. He told us that he had seen him earlier that morning. When he said this, my heart did happy flips, but I made him repeat himself because I wanted to make sure that I heard him correctly. He said, "Yes, I saw him here this morning getting gas." Then he told me that when Hicks left, he headed back up Highway Number Nine. The attendant pointed out the direction; pointing back up towards Hicks's sister's house where we had just left. After we got the news, we were so relieved, and so we headed for home since we thought that he was okay. Thinking back, we didn't even go back to tell his mom what we had found out. I guess we were too exhausted because we had been up all night and almost all that day, and just wanted to go home and go to bed to get some sleep. Now thinking back, I'm glad that we didn't because it would have been nothing but false information.

I woke up late that Saturday night, and I still had not heard from or seen Hicks. I contemplated calling his uncle to see if he would tell me where he was. I pondered this thought for a while then I told my mom what I was considering. My mom said, "Girl, you better just leave that man alone, you know he ain't gonna tell you where Hicks is." I sat up the rest of the night wondering where Hicks was, and where could he have gone after he left the gas station. I stayed up waiting for him to call or come by until my eyes grew tired. I knew that he had disappeared before and came back, so I went on to bed thinking that I would see him the next day. That Sunday morning, Hicks still hadn't shown up, nor had he called. My family and I got dressed and went to church, and was there until twelve thirty p.m. When we got home, Hicks still had not surfaced. I had hoped to see his car sitting in the yard with him waiting in it or him on the porch. When I got out of the car, I looked down at the ground to see if there were any signs of his car's tire tracks, but there wasn't. I went into the house and fell across the bed and pondered where he could possibly be. I didn't know whether to cry or scream or be sad or angry. However, I did tell myself that if Hicks showed up, I would be so happy to see him that I wouldn't even fuss at him, but I would tell him that he should have at least called to check on his daughter. My mom opened the bedroom door and interrupted my train of thought. She told me that she was about to go out for a bit with her friend and asked if I wanted to go. I told her that I was too tired and would stay there and wait on Hicks. She told me okay and closed the door. A few minutes later, I heard her friend's horn and the front door closing. My siblings also prepared to leave the house, but before they did; they asked me if they could take my daughter with them because our grandmother had called and asked to see her great grandbaby. I was now in the house all alone, and it was so quiet that I could hear the buzz of the electrical currents flowing through the house. I yelled out, "Hicks, where are you!" I then got up and went and sat by the phone and waited, hoping that Hicks would call, but he never did.

My mom got back home around 9:00 p.m., and asked had I heard anything from Hicks, and I sadly told her no. She then asked where everyone was, and I told her at our grandmothers, and said that everyone would probably spend the night there. My mom sat down, and I could tell that she had something on her mine, so I asked, "What is it Momma?" My mom looked at me then dropped her head, and then told me how she and her friend had passed Hicks's uncle's house. She said that as they were about to pass by the house, she asked her friend if she could slow down, so she could see if anything seemed out of the ordinary. My mom paused and said that all I could see was a dark house with a dim glow coming from the basement area. She looked me in my eyes and said, "I got a bad feeling that Hicks was in that basement, and I believe that he may be dead."

When my mom said what she said, it made my heart skip a beat, and tears welled up in my chest and poured from my eyes. My mom's positivity had kept me going. She had reassured me that night at work that I would be o.k., and that Hicks was o.k. that morning when he didn't pick us up from work. But now, there she sat depleted of any hope for my young husband. When she told me her thoughts and feelings, her words hit me like daggers to my heart, and it tore me apart. My mom didn't stop, her words and thoughts continued to pour out like a broken floodgate. I guess she had been holding her thoughts in all day, but she was now finally ready to give me my reality check. She told me that there was something else that she saw as she was coming back home, and she found it puzzling and suspicious. She paused and was now looking at me with great concern because I had started to snatch small puffs of air, I could barely breathe. My tears were pouring down my face like a flowing river and were being collected by my shirt like a sponge, and I could feel myself screaming in my throat even though there was no sound coming out. My mom looked as if she was afraid to continue, but I told her to go ahead with her story. She resumed and said that after she and her friend left their outing, they passed by the local funeral home and saw a crane sitting in front of it. I whispered through my tears, "You mean a wrecker?" I had now lost my voice from sobbing and could barely speak above a whisper. She said, "No, a crane." Puzzle by this too, I attempted to describe to her what she had seen. I told her that she probably saw the truck that carries the grave stones and vaults. She looked at me and said, "I know what I saw!" She then described it to me further and told me how tall it was, and after she finished, I knew that it was indeed a crane. My mom then asked, "Why would a funeral home need something like that?" I whispered that I didn't know. My mom and I continued to talk well into the morning. Although, she had given me her thoughts on Hicks, and what she believed happened to him, I still waited on a call from him. I prayed that it would be the same scenario as before; where he was gone for three days and then returned home. After staying up so long, our eyes finally grew heavy, so we went to bed.

The Monday morning sun unwelcomely burst through my bedroom window, and it woke me up. In addition to the sun, the noise from the hustle and bustle of my siblings preparing for school, also played a part in my sleep disturbance. I looked over and found my daughter next to me deep in sleep. I stared at her and listened to her little breaths as her chest rose and fell. She looked so at peace, and I found myself wondering if she had noticed that she had not seen her dad. Then I started to think about what if we both never saw him again, and how this would affect her if that happened. Tears started to swell my throat again, but I fought them back. My daughter had never asked where her dad was, but I had noticed that every time my mom and I spoke about him, she would stare at us and listen in on our conversation. At the time, she was almost three years old, and could speak very well, but her dad was never one of her topics. It was almost as if she already knew where he was and was just waiting for us to figure it out. When the subject of Hicks closed, she would go back to playing or doing whatever she was doing before. As I stared at her closed fluttering lids, I wondered if Hicks was visiting her in her dreams, and since she was so young maybe this was why she didn't realize that she had not seen him.

I eased out of the bed and bed-room and went and sat on the couch. My eyes were swollen slits, and my throat was raw. I sat silently on the couch trying to see if I could hear the gravelly sound of Hicks tires on the dirt road, or the roar of his engine in the distance. My mom joined me on the couch but said nothing. My dad was getting dressed for work and didn't say anything to me. He knew that I had been crying, and I guess he didn't want to say anything to make me start back. After he left for work, my mom decided that she would go back to bed and suggested that I do the same. I then hoarsely whispered that I couldn't sleep because I was too worried. My mom got up off the couch then said, "I know you are." She then touched my shoulder as she passed me on her way back to her bedroom.

Around 9:00 a.m., I heard a car coming up the hill, so I jumped up and ran to the door. I went out on the porch trying to see the car before it got to the house. I knew it wasn't Hicks's car, so I wanted to see who it was just in case it was the white car again that had chased us previously. It was another car that I didn't recognize, and it slowly came up the hill and turned into the driveway. I ran back in the house and told my mother. She got up, took a gun from the gun rack, and passed it to me. She also prepared herself for the possible confrontation. I peeped out the door, watching the car fully come up in the yard. The driver parked close to the house and honked the horn. The horn was loud and obnoxious, and the person in the car held it down longer than they should have. I cracked the door while holding the shotgun at my side. There were two men in the car, and they were talking to each other in a low muffled voice. When the driver and his companion turned to look at the house through the car window that was partially down, they saw me standing in the door. I didn't know who they were, but heard the driver muffle out words to me through the partially opened car window. Since I could not hear what was said, I forced my voice to yell, "What do you want!" The driver of the car then rolled the window all the way down, and I saw that it was another one of Hicks's uncles and his brother. When I saw them, I turned and told my mom who they were, and she relaxed. She came and got my gun and put it away and didn't bother coming back out. I stepped out of the doorway, went to the edge the porch, and looked at the car. Hicks's brother and uncle remained in the car but leaned over and looked at me. Hicks's uncle then told me the most devastating news that I could have ever imagined, and when he said it, it sent waves of pain through my entire body. In a very deep southern voice and dry tone, I heard his uncle say, "They done found James Edwards up on Number 9 dead in his car." I gasped and painfully swallowed my spit, and said through hoarse vocal cords, "Dead, dead how?" His uncle responded, "We don't know, we just know they said that he was dead." I started crying and banging my fists on the railing of the porch, and slightly above a whisper said, "I tried to tell him that they were going to kill him, I tried to tell him, but he wouldn't listen." I was waiting for them to exit the car to give me more information, or at least console me, but the uncle fired up the car's engine, backed out of the driveway, and then left. Never saying sorry for your loss, come up to the house, bye, or nothing.

9.

TILL DEATH DO US PART

I STAYED OUT ON THE PORCH for a while trying to pull myself together before I went back in to tell my mom what happened. When I entered, she was sitting on the couch and asked, "What did those two want?" When I looked at her with tears streaming down my face, she stood up, walked over to me, and said, "What?" I collapsed on her shoulder and said, "Momma, they just told me that Hicks was found dead in his car up on Highway 9." She rubbed and patted me on my back like a baby, and we wept in each other's arms. She then asked me what I was going to do, and I told her that I didn't know. I waited for her to suggest something, but at the time she was just as upset as I was, and we both were scared. My daughter woke up and came into the living room, and when she saw us crying, she stood there staring at us. She then walked over to me and raised her arms for me to pick her up. After I scooped her up, she laid her head on my chest as if to comfort me; never saying a word. I sat down on the couch with her and sobbed. My daughter would periodically look up at me, and then would lay her head back down on my chest. I could feel her little hand rubbing up and down my rib cage and patting them as she sat in my lap. After a while, my tears slowed. When the tears stopped, my chest grabbed small puffs of air, as my heart and lungs were trying to return to normal. My daughter then looked up at me and said, "You alright momma, you be okay, don't cry no more." Her statement made the floodgates reopen, and my tears ignited again. My mom walked over and took my daughter from my lap and told her that it was time for breakfast. My daughter quickly forgot about her crying mother and yelled out to her grandma what she wanted to eat, and they disappeared into the kitchen. I could hear them chattering from behind the kitchen door but could not make out what they were saying. I sat there thinking about my next move and was still at a loss. I decided to clean myself up and get dressed and hoped this would make me feel better. After I bathed and dressed, I looked at myself in the mirror. My eyes were still very swollen, and my throat felt like I had swallowed razor blades. I then decided that I wasn't going to cry anymore, and that I was going to be strong for me and for my baby.

A few hours later, I heard the school bus tires squeak to a stop, and my siblings came running in excited about their day. Their laughter stopped when I entered the living room, and they immediately began asking me what was wrong. I could barely speak, so my mom broke the news to them. When she told them, it was as if they were all shot at once with one bullet, because they all fell to the floor screaming and crying. My younger brothers took it the hardest because Hicks spent a lot of time with them. He would drive them around or let them drive. Plus, he would let them watch or assist him when he made car repairs. They cried and cried, and when my dad came home, they were still crying. When he came in from work, he saw how upset everyone was, and asked what was wrong. When we told him, my dad got upset too, and said, "Lord have mercy, it's a pity and a shame that they killed that boy like that!" I couldn't take it anymore, so I got up and went to my room, and fell across the bed so I could cry alone, but I was all cried out.

As the news circulated throughout the small community, people started to show up at my parent's house to give their condolences. I was still in my room as the groups poured in; each having a different story to tell about Hicks and his uncle the preacher. As I prepared myself to come out of my room to face everyone, I was suddenly stopped in my steps by what I heard, and it scared me. The voices from the living room sounded just like the ones that I had heard that Friday night at the plant, and the memory made me feel weak. I stood there and tried to compose myself and my thoughts, but the reality of it all was hitting me all at once. I felt a strong urge to stay in the room, but I needed to see who the voices were connected to. When I came out of my room, I saw familiar faces with eyes that anxiously waited for me and my reaction. I faked my strength and walked into the room. I said hello to everyone and thanked them for coming to see me. I'm sure they thought that I was going to tarry with them, and offer information that they did not have, but I quickly said goodbye and immediately returned to my room.

When I left the room, it was silent for a bit and then the chatter returned. I walked back to my bed and crawled back into my original position and listened to the cluttered conversations. Suddenly, I thought about the other voice I'd heard that night at work. I replayed the words and the sound of it over again in my mind. "Hey, Mary Dean!" When I did, it made me sick to my stomach, and I had a strong urge to throw up. I then knew exactly who that voice belonged to, it was Hicks. My heart was heavy again, and I started to weep uncontrollably, but silently to myself. I believe Hicks was tortured that night, and as he was dying, he was calling out to me before his spirit left his body and the earth. The thought of it all devastated me and I could no longer fight back my tears, but with my tears I began to get very angry.

Hicks latter teenage years and early twenties were spent going to work, working on his cars, or being an errand boy for his uncle. Everyone seemed to like him, so I wanted to know why someone would hurt a young man in his prime, and one who they knew had a wife and small child. When Hicks's uncle's wives were killed, I heard tales of how he was taking out insurance policies on family members, and then murdering them to collect the money. The information was circulating around the community and in local newspapers, so I had no choice but to also believe that Hicks was another one of his uncle's victims. In my heart, I believed that he was responsible, and was the culprit or mastermind behind Hicks's death, and this infuriated me. He had finally succeeded at keeping us apart.

The next day, I grabbed my gun, borrowed my parent's car, and went to Hicks's mom's house. I chose an earlier time to go because I knew that a large majority of the spectators would be at work. When I got there, to my surprise, Hicks's uncle's car was there. I almost turned around, but remembered I had my gun. I parked and went up to the door and knocked. One of Hicks siblings came to the door and let me in. When I entered, I saw an empty living room, but heard voices coming from a back bedroom. I was escorted to the room, it was the bedroom Hicks and I had once shared when we lived with his family. When I entered the room, I saw Hicks mother, grandmother, siblings, and uncles. Most of all, I saw his uncle, the preacher. It appeared as if he was conducting the family meeting, and everyone was crying except him. I stood wondering why the meeting was in a back bedroom instead of the living room. Later I thought about it, and I figured that Hicks's uncle didn't want anyone listening in on the meeting from the front porch.

I was invited into the room and given a chair. The chair was placed right next to Hicks's uncle the preacher. When I took my seat, he resumed his lecture. The first thing he said was, "Yawl need to hurry up and put that boy in the ground." When he said this, everyone in the room lost it, and started moaning and crying. This seemed to upset Hicks's uncle, and he said, "Whatcha crying fa?" "He dead now, and ya crying ain't gonna bring him back!" I stared at his blank uncaring face and I could feel my blood began to boil. He then turned and looked at me, and for the first time he looked in to my eyes and said, "What yawl waiting fa?" My eyes were squinting and twitching in anger. He removed his evil eyes from me, and looked around the room and said again, "Yawl need to hurry up and put that boy in the ground!" I spoke up and said, "He just died!" My voice was still hoarse, but I used it to the best of its ability; wishing it could have been louder. He stared down at me with soulless eyes that didn't care, and I followed up my first response with, "And, I don't even have anything to wear!" Hicks's uncle looked down at me with controlling hateful eyes, and in a deep country snarl said, "Wear whatcha got on!" At the time, I was in blue jeans and a tee shirt, and couldn't believe his audacity to suggest what apparel I should wear to my own husband's funeral. He stood there and blatantly showed disrespect for me, my husband, and the family. He was basically telling me and the family that Hicks was worthless. How dare he suggest a meager attire for me at my husband's funeral, when he himself walked around in three-piece suits just to cut wood. I thought, "He's trying to disrespect my husband even in death." He sat in his seat which was right next to mine, as if he had spoken and his word was final. His words and behavior made me want to remove the gun from my purse and kill him right there in front of the family. I felt the imprint of the gun in my purse, and something was whispering to me, "Kill him, kill him." Those whispers turned to screams when I stared up in to his evil eyes and saw them looking back down at me. To fight the screams in my head, I yelled out as loud as I could muster with my hoarse voice, "I don't wanna wear what I got on!" Then I stared him down until he could no longer hold eye contact with me. I don't know what he saw, but he quickly removed his eyes from me, and stormed out of the room.

Hicks's family quietly watched our interaction, and once he left the room they began to talk. When he was completely out of the room, and I could no longer hear his footsteps going down the hallway, I turned and asked them who was it that found Hicks. His brother answered and said, "Someone called and reported it." He told me that the caller told 911 that they had seen the sun reflecting off the windshield of a wrecked car when they came down Highway Nine. The caller was a woman and had made the call early that morning. I asked them if they knew the name of the woman, but nobody knew.

On that February morning when Hicks was found, it had been raining, and it was very dark and hazy. We discussed how impossible it would have been for the caller to have seen the sun reflecting off Hicks's windshield because there was no sun that day. The sky had been blanketed with dark clouds and rain, so this puzzled all of us. I then asked the family where the car was found, and his brother responded again and said, "Off of Highway Number Nine under an embankment." I thought silently for a moment, and then I asked, "Did this embankment have white sand and pretty streaming water?" Hicks's brother answered, "Yes it did, how did you know that?" His family watched with complete interest as I told them that Hicks had taken me there, and he told me how it was his favorite place to play as a child when he'd visit his uncle's house. As a matter of fact, his uncle's old house was right across the road from the place where Hicks's car was found.

Hicks's family stared at me in silence, and I could tell they knew all about where their brother and uncle once lived. However, I don't believe that they knew about Hicks's special place. His special place ended up being his final place, and the person who put him there knew all about it. Hicks's brother spoke up, and he said that it was true that his uncle once lived across the road from where Hicks's car was found. When he confirmed it, I thought to myself, "Surely now the family know that this was no accident."

Hicks had taken me to his childhood spot on a date. It was down a steep ravine which he had to help me down. He went down first then guided me to him. Once we got down the ravine, we walked along a small beach with white sands. He introduced me to it and told me about his fun-happy times playing there alone. When it was time for us to go, he climbed the ravine first then helped me back up. I was sitting there thinking about all of this when my flashback was interrupted by Hicks's brother telling us how Hicks body looked when it was recovered. I was expecting to hear that Hicks and his car was mangled beyond recognition, but instead I heard that the car was pulled from the ravine in one piece. When I heard this, I quickly realized that it was no way his car could have possibly driven down there and not been smashed to pieces, so it had to have been placed there. I sat there evaluating everything I was hearing and had heard his brother say. I kept quiet and didn't show any facial expression or emotion as I processed the information. When I was done, I thought to myself. "So that's why... that's why the large crane was needed!"

Hicks's brother continued to tell what he'd seen when the car was recovered. He said Hicks was behind the wheel and his arms were locked to his chest as if he'd been praying. One leg was over the console while the other was under the steering wheel. Hicks's brother said that once Hicks's body was removed, he looked around inside the car. He noticed that the car key was bent inside the ignition switch, and said it looked purposely done. He then got out and looked in to the trunk, and saw clothing that consisted of a red shirt, blue jeans, and pair of sneakers, and he said that they were all wet. He paused, and then looked as if he was choosing his words wisely before he said them. He swallowed then said, "I also looked under his hood, and the car had been stripped of everything including the motor." I gasped and said, "The motor!" "How can a car wreck with no motor?" He answered, "I don't know, but that's what I saw with my own eyes."

I couldn't take anymore, so I got up and went outside. His sister that lived in the home Hicks and I once shared came out and talked to me. She said to me, "I'm glad you stood up to uncle." She then told me that her uncle had been at their house ever since Hicks body was found, and said that everyone wishes he would just leave, so we can have a moment to grieve. I asked her if he had spent the night there. She told me he hadn't but was there until everyone went to bed before he would leave. She said he stayed so long that he was even the one who locked the front door. We hurried up and went back inside because I knew he was watching us. I didn't want her to get in trouble for talking to me outside of the house. I stayed about another hour, and then decided it was time for me to go. I got in my mom's car and said a prayer to God asking him to protect me on my way back home. I remember being afraid I'd be followed, or a roadblock would be set up for me. I was afraid at every turn but kept replaying what my daddy had told me to do. He told me, "If anyone tries to stop you, shoot them in the damn head!" "Kill the head, kill the body!" I made it home safely but was still very uneasy. I was uneasy because I knew I would have to do the trip all over again the very next day because the family and I were going to go together to pick out Hicks's casket. I got nauseous every time I thought about my schedule and dreaded how fast the time seemed to be passing.

The next morning, there was a knock on my parent's door. When I opened it, there stood a middle-aged white police officer. I asked him how I could help him, and he asked if he could speak to the wife of James Hicks. I told him he was speaking to her. He then asked if I could come down to the police station in Rockford, AL and give a statement. I asked when he would like me to go there. He replied, "Now, would be fine," and appeared to wait for me. I told him I'd drive myself, and he said okay. He returned to his car but waited on me. I borrowed my mother's car and followed him to the police department. When I got there, I was asked to take a seat and told that an investigator would be with me shortly. As I waited, I felt happy and so relieved that someone was actually looking into my husband's death. I was on pins and needles and could hardly wait to tell what I knew and had heard. After waiting for a few minutes, the investigator called me in to his office. When I got to the open door, I peeped in and saw a Country Hick sitting behind the desk with the nastiest smirk on his face. He asked me to have a seat. He immediately started asking me questions about

Hicks, but I noticed he wasn't writing anything down or even attempting to take notes. The first question he asked me was if my husband smoked weed. I looked at him in disbelief, and answered, "No, I have never seen him smoke anything." He then asked me if he drank. I told him, "Yes, occasionally, but Hicks was not a real drinker." I then told him that when Hicks bought alcohol, it was usually just to give to his friends. The investigator then asked me if I knew Hicks's uncle. I said, "I don't know him, but I've seen him on several occasions." Then all a sudden the investigator stood up and said, "Okay then, if we come up with anything more, we'll call you." I sat there staring at the investigator in disbelief; immediately realizing how coming there had been a waste of time. Thinking back, I believe he was paid off just like the others. He was just questioning me to see how much I knew, and if I was dumb enough to share what I knew with him.

After I left the police department, I went to Hicks's family's house, so we could go to the funeral home to pick out his casket, and then funeral outfits. When we arrived at the funeral home, the funeral home director was already expecting us. He was standing in the door watching us as we got out of the car. He welcomed us in, and he seemed to be the happiest funeral home director I'd ever seen. Instead of being compassionate and sorrowful, he acted as if we were his dinner guests; invited to his home for a celebration. He was grinning like a Cheshire Cat, and acted like he wanted to break out a bottle of champagne to celebrate our grief. His behavior was so out of line that it brought one of Hicks's sisters to uncontrollable tears. She finally said, "What the hell is so funny!" "What are you laughing at because we don't see a damn thing funny!" Hicks's mother tried to calm her down and had to restrain her because she was getting ready to hit him. After Hicks's sister finished cursing him out, he became embarrassed and angry, and didn't want to assist us anymore with the casket selection. When we asked him a question, he waved his hand and said, "Yawl can choose one of them over there." He then sat down at his desk and stared at us with impatient eyes. He now seemed as if he wanted us to leave his dinner party that he once acted like we came to enjoy.

We quickly chose a casket and left, and I can't tell you to this day what color casket I chose. What is most memorable is that the cost for the casket was never mentioned. I didn't have any money to bury him, and neither did his mom since his death was still under investigation, and this prevented the insurance claim from being paid. I silently pondered to myself, "Who is going to pay for all of this…who has the money?" Then I heard these statements ring out loudly in my head, "Hurry up and put that boy in the ground!" "Whatcha waiting on?" "Whatcha crying fa?" "He's dead now and crying ain't gonna bring him back!"

After we left the funeral home, we went shopping for our funeral attire. We chose yellow as our color theme because it symbolized friendship. Although Hicks was no longer with us, his sisters and I had agreed we'd always be family. We already had a bond, but the blood of Hicks's offspring completely sealed our covenant. We finished shopping, and when we returned to the family house, I didn't tarry. I got in my parent's car and quickly and fearfully drove home. Thinking back, one of my family members was always with me when I was afraid and needed to go somewhere; either my mom or my brother. Although I was terrified, for some reason, I never asked either one of them to come with me to Hicks's family's house.

Thursday evening of that same week, we had Hicks wake and viewing. It was held at the funeral home of the once overly happy director. I went there with Hicks's family, and my family was to join us later. When we arrived, the director told the family that my daughter and I would be first to view the body. When we walked in to the viewing area where his casket sat, the funeral director closed two thick velvety red curtains behind us, and he stayed on the outside of them. I picked up my daughter and held her in my arms and walked towards the casket. I felt weak and nervous walking up the aisle towards it. My knees wanted to buckle under me, and I fought the urge to let them. This would be the first time I saw Hicks since he left work that Friday night. The mere thought of him now lying in the box before me made me feel hollow and nauseated. I really didn't want to see him but knew I would regret it if I didn't. As I slowly walked towards the casket, I thought about our last hug and our last kiss that we had given each other. I also thought about how I had watched him anxiously walk toward the exit doors of the plant, and his speed while walking. If only he had known that he was speed walking to his own demise. As I neared the casket, I thought about our last conversation where he talked about wanting us to have another child, so our daughter wouldn't have to grow up alone. Did he somehow know that his time on earth was about to end? However, what I thought about most of all was our conversation where he told me about his biggest wish, and that was to see family he had not seen in a long time, and to have a family reunion. I pushed back tears thinking about how his wish was coming true, but he wouldn't be alive to see it nor enjoy it. It didn't seem fair, and I blamed myself for not being more aggressive in making him listen.

Finally, we had made our way up the aisle and was standing directly in front of the casket. When I looked down into it and upon Hicks's face, I barely recognized him. His skin color had darkened, and his face and eyes were swollen; even his head looked swollen. When I saw how swollen his head was, I immediately tried to examine it. I separated his hair down to his scalp to see if it could help me determine why his head looked so big. When I parted his hair, his scalped was riddled with silver staples that appeared to keep his scalp together. I then opened a few buttons on his shirt to see if I could see any injuries to his chest. When I did, I saw silver paper under it, and it completely covered his chest. When I looked back up at his head, I saw that his hair was combed, but it still contained small particles of debris that looked like dirt and straw. My eyes traveled down his body searching for imperfections. When I got to his hands, they were crossed on his chest, and I saw that his knuckles were bruised. His fingers curved as if they once made fists, and his fingernails were filthy. I asked Hicks as if he could answer, "What did they do to you my husband, how did they kill you?"

I leaned over and started rubbing his arm, and said to my daughter, "Look at your dad?" She turned and looked at him as a child looks at a sleeping parent. She stared at him as if she was waiting for him to wake up; not understanding that he would never open his eyes again to look at her. I told her to give her dad a kiss, and I leaned her over into the casket and watched as she kissed him lightly on the forehead. I then leaned over and kissed him on the forehead as well. I began to cry, and I said to him, "Hicks, why didn't you listen to me?" "Why didn't you listen, I tried to tell you they were going to kill you!" I continued to talk to him and rub his head until the funeral director came in and stopped me. He appeared from nowhere and grabbed my hand and told me I couldn't touch the body. I snatched away my hand, and stared at him and thought, "If, you don't take your damn hands off of me!" It was as if the funeral director read my mind because he quickly let go of my hand and got the hell out of that room.

Soon, my daughter became restless in my arms, and wiggled down out of them. When her feet touched the floor, she took off running and headed towards the closed velvety red curtains that separated the room from the waiting area. She'd heard the voices of various family members waiting outside the room, so she raced down the aisle towards them. I gave Hicks another quick look then headed down the aisle to catch up with her. When she got to the curtains, I was right behind her when she opened them and slipped through. Hicks's uncle the preacher was the first face I saw when I came through the curtains. He had placed a folding chair right next to the curtain's entrance while everyone else sat further away in the pews. I believe he chose this location so he would be able to hear everything said by family and friends viewing Hicks's body.

When my daughter went through the curtains and entered the room, Hicks's uncle reached over and tried to quickly grab her up as she entered. His hands were just as quickly slapped away by my dad, who Hicks's uncle didn't realize had come and stood to his blindside. As my dad slapped away his hands he said, "Nigga, don't you touch her!" My dad then moved to the front of him and stood staring down at him in the folding chair. Hicks's uncle didn't move, and I believe it was due to pure shock because he didn't see it coming. He gazed up at my dad as he said, "As a matter of fact, don't you ever touch my grandbaby!" The room went silent, and everyone listened as my dad made a blatant threat. He said, "Don't make me kill you, because I will... Will!" You could hear a rat peeing on cotton, and nobody said a word or moved because my crazy crazed dad had the floor. He then said, "You can kill everybody in your whole got damn family if you want, but if anything happens to my daughter or to my grandbaby; I will lay out in your yard waiting for you to come home, and will blow your so and so head off, and I mean that!" I quickly looked around and saw shocked eyes gazing upon my dad as he held the spotlight. My dad was showing everyone he was not afraid, and he was going to protect his family. My mom nervously got up from the pew where she was sitting and tried to calm my dad down. She tried her best to talk low enough so no one would hear her. I heard her begging my dad not to make a scene in front of all those people. My dad paid my mom no mind, and loudly said, "To hell with all of these people because I know what I'm going to do to him, if he hurt my daughter or granddaughter!" My mom slightly tugged at his shirt trying to break his stare and hovering posture over Hicks's uncle. My dad ignored her and said, "Folks been letting him get away with all this killing around here, and ain't nobody trying to stop him, but I'm gonna stop him tonight!"

Hicks's uncle sat there like a knot on a log, and to me he looked like a child that had been punished and sent to time out, or a cat that had been caught with the canary in its mouth. He was too afraid to even blink, and the consequence was standing right in front of him. My dad was grinding his teeth and biting his lip. He often did this when he got angry, or as my mom would say, "When he got Hell in him." My dad stood there and continued to give Hicks's uncle his death stare, and that was when I saw his hand go in to his pocket. My momma yelled out, "Don't do that… don't pull that gun out in here!" When my dad pulled his hand from his pocket, the gun fell out and onto the floor. He quickly picked it up and held it pointed towards the floor with his finger on the trigger. As he held it in his hand, he continued his death stare, and then asked me without looking over at me, "Just say the word Sugga Momma, just say the word." When I heard his question, I whispered to him in my still hoarse voice to stop. I wanted justice but didn't want to see my dad go to jail. When my dad's lips started trembling, I knew then how serious he was about his question. I said, "Daddy please now, don't do it?" The preacher sat motionless waiting for my dad's decision. He had started to sweat, and as he sat still in the folding chair, I saw small beads of sweat running down his neck from behind his ears.

My mom called out my dad's name, and told him that she was ready to go, but my dad didn't move. It was only after hearing the bells that jingled above the funeral home's door, did my dad come from his trance. One of my brothers opened it, and the bells seemed to bring my dad back to reality. When he came to himself, he said, "Yeah, I better go, it's time to go." He sounded as if he was trying to convince himself. My dad put the gun back in his pocket, turned, and headed for the door. When I looked over at my brothers, I saw them looking as if they were standing guard until my dad fully exited the parlor. After he was fully out of the door, my two younger brothers followed him while my two older brothers waited behind. They stayed behind guarding my dad, while waiting for my mom. They looked like a small army of men.

When I saw my family leaving, I grabbed up my daughter and left with them. Although it was my husband's wake, his uncle's presence drove me and my family away early. We couldn't tolerate seeing him there when we believed he was the reason Hicks was dead. In fact, after watching Hicks's family, and several people from the community who I knew had said bad things about Hicks's uncle; smiling in his face and saying, "Hello Reverend" while giving condolences to him, it made me realized that I couldn't trust anyone except my family. My original intentions and plan were to go back to the family's house after the wake, and spend time with Hicks's family, but when I told my dad, he didn't think it was a good idea. He even told me that if it wouldn't be a shame, he wouldn't even let me go to the funeral. My mom agreed with him, and honestly, I did too. I really didn't want to go to the funeral because seeing Hicks in his casket at his wake was enough for me, but I knew it would look bad if I didn't show up.

That Friday, a week from the day Hicks had disappeared; we held his funeral. The morning of the funeral, I woke up in pure disgust because I knew I'd have to say goodbye to him for good. I dreaded the fact that I would have to return to the family house where everyone seemed nervous and too scared to speak about Hicks's death. I hated that I would have to keep a straight face while looking at the man who wanted to put my husband in the ground the same day after his body was found. Out of all the reasons, it pained me the most knowing that he had finally succeeded in keeping Hicks and I apart.

The morning of the funeral, the plan was to meet at the family house with my daughter, so we could ride in the family limo. Someone from my family would have to drive me there, and it ended up being my Great Uncle George. He was from Gadsden, Alabama, and came in to town for the funeral. I was so glad to see my uncle because he was one of my favorites who I didn't get to see often. He was a handsome six-foot-tall bi-racial man that was always well groomed and dressed. For a man in his early sixties, he was in great shape. He had served many years in the U.S. Navy and still jogged and worked out, so he had a muscular build which made him look much younger than he was. My family was still getting dressed, so I took him up on his offer to drive me to Hicks's family home. My mom told me to leave my daughter with her. She saw that I was a nervous wreck, and barely knew what to do with my own self. Plus, I didn't know what to expect or what was going to happen once I got there.

When my uncle and I neared the family home, he asked if he could come in because he personally wanted to meet Hicks's uncle. He told me how the news about him had traveled all the way to Gadsden, Alabama, and when he heard it, he couldn't believe that it was only one man that was loose in the small community that he had also grown up in. He then opened his sport coat and showed me his gun. When I saw this, I felt relieved because I was carrying a small purse that my gun couldn't fit in.

When we turned in to the driveway, the family cars were all lined up. Hicks's uncle's car was first. My uncle quickly parked, and he then walked me to the door. The door was open, so I opened the screen and we walked in. When we entered the house, the preacher was sitting in a big chair in the living room by himself. His legs were crossed with his ankle resting on top of his knee. His legs made the number four. He looked very comfortable and relaxed. As I looked at him, I noticed that one of his pant legs were up, and it exposed his sock. On top of his sock and around his ankle, I saw a string with four tarnished and dull silver bells on it. The bells looked like the ones found on a baby's walking shoe, but they were much larger. When I saw them, I couldn't help but stare. I wondered why a grown man would wear something like this. When he saw me staring at them, he immediately tried to pull his pant leg down over them, and I could tell that my staring at them made him very uncomfortable, and that he had never meant for me to see them. He then covered them with his hand. When he covered them, I looked back up into his face, and found his eyes staring back at me; they were piercing and mean.

I was caught up in the piercing stare, that is when I felt a touch from my uncle's hand, and it made me break my gaze. When I turned and looked at my uncle, I found that he had taken my place in the stare down. When I turned back around to reface Hicks's uncle, I noticed that he had also changed his focus, and was now in a stare down with my uncle. I broke their quiet icicle stares by introducing them to each other. I said, "This is my uncle George from Gadsden." Hicks's uncle quickly leaped from the big chair and extended his hand towards my uncle. My uncle continued to stare at him, and then folded his arms. When this happened, Hicks's uncle withdrew his hand and sat back down. I watched in amusement as he uncomfortably twisted and turned in the chair that he once looked so comfortable and relaxed in. I knew it was because of my uncle's unwavering stare, and unfriendly folded arms.

Suddenly, one of Hicks's sisters appeared in the doorway and said, "I thought I heard your voice." She then asked me to join her and the rest of the ladies who were in her mom's bedroom in the back of the house. After she said this, she disappeared from the door, and I heard her footsteps heading back towards the room. I told my uncle to have a seat and left him with Hicks's uncle. As I made my way down the narrow hallway heading back to the room, I had a smirk on my face. Hicks had told me that his uncle had once been in the Army, so I found it funny that the Army and Navy were now in one room, and they were in a staring war with each other.

When I made it to the bedroom at the back of the house, Hicks's mom and siblings were sitting around talking. To my surprise, one of my aunts was in the room too. She was my mom's sister. When I saw my aunt, I was glad to see her, but wanted to know why she was at the house. When I asked her, she told me that Hicks would sometimes drop our daughter off with her when he had something to do. When she told me this, I knew it was another one of Hicks's little secrets. However, when she told me, something came to me. I had visited my aunt with my daughter one day, and after talking and shooting the breeze with her; my aunt got up and went to her record player and said, "Watch this?" My aunt put on a song, and when she did, my daughter leaped from the couch and started dancing. My aunt and I laughed and laughed. I then asked my aunt how she knew my daughter liked it and would dance to it. My aunt just laughed but wouldn't tell me. Now seeing her at the family house, I knew why.

When I tuned back in to Hicks's mom and his siblings' conversation, they were discussing some type of calming medicine that one sister had gotten from the pharmacy. I sat down and listened as they discussed the dosage, and how we should all take some of the medicine to keep our nerves calm during the funeral. I immediately told them that I didn't want any of the medicine. Hicks's sister then said that if anyone needed it, it would be me. She then coaxed me into taking it. I gave in but told them that I would only take a little bit because I didn't know what it was, or how I would react to it. It was a clear liquid with no smell or taste, but as soon as I took it, I felt calm. His sisters and mom took some too, but one of his cousins refused. She told us that she didn't believe it would help her and said that she wasn't going to take it. Hicks's baby sister warned her, and said she was going to wish she had once she got to the funeral. She refused, and so we ignored her then prepared to leave for the funeral.

When we walked back to the living room, both uncles were still sitting quietly. I introduced my uncle to everyone, and he said hello. Once he saw that I was securely with the rest of the family, he stood up and said that he would see me at the church. He looked over at Hicks's uncle and squinted his eyes into a frown. Hicks's uncle looked at him, but quickly looked away and pretended to be focusing on something on the floor. When my uncle exited out the screen door, and the preacher heard the screen door slam, he quickly looked up and appeared to be making sure that my uncle was really leaving. His eyes quickly found me, and I was already staring at him, and this made him look away again, and he dropped his head.

We were all in the living room like a miniature herd, when a knock came on the screen door and startled us. We looked towards the door and saw the funeral director coming through it. He told us it was getting time to load up and go. After he said this, Hicks's mom suggested that we say a prayer before we departed. The funeral director asked all the men standing on the porch to come into the house. When the men entered the house, Hicks's uncle stood up from the chair he was in and volunteered to lead us all in prayer. I heard his southern drawl voice say, "Everybody bow ya heads." I looked around to see what everyone was about to do. I then saw the men as well as Hicks's mom and siblings bowing their heads with their eyes closed, and they were waiting for Hicks's uncle's prayer. I looked at them in disbelief. Were they really going to let the man they knew was responsible for Hicks's death pray over him? Tears welled up in my eyes and throat, and I felt like I couldn't breathe. I felt like I needed to scream to the top of my voice to release the pressure that build up. My chest was so heavy that I ran out of the house; letting the screen door slam behind me. At that moment, my biggest regret was that I had let my uncle leave me there. If he had not, I believe that I would have asked him to take me home.

When Hicks's family came out of the house, they looked at me as if I were crazy. I looked back at them in anger, but mostly pity because they were too afraid to stand up for themselves, and for their dead love ones. Hicks's sister; the one that lived in our house, walked over to me, and placed her arm on my shoulder, and nudged me towards the waiting limos. We were directed to the first limo, and inside of it would contain Hicks's mom, his two older sisters, and me. To my surprise, I found out that our limo would be led by Hicks's uncle instead of the funeral director. I had noticed his car parked in the front of the limos earlier when my uncle and I arrived, but I had no clue that he would be the leader of the procession. I got angry, and no longer wanted to be in the first limo because I didn't want to look at the back of his head. Plus, I felt that the only place he should have been was in jail. So many thoughts were running through my mind as I sat in the back of that limo, and I thought about all the unwelcomed surprises I had endured from the day. First, seeing the uncle when I entered the house, him leading prayer over my dead husband, and now leading the family to my husband's funeral; whom I believe he was responsible for the death of. But with all those surprises, I was surprised most by the car he decided to drive. Hicks's uncle had several nice cars, but the day of the funeral, he chose the ugliest one he had. It was an old ugly brown Lincoln, and its dustiness and dirtiness made it look even worse. I thought, "At least he could have washed that car to make it look a little better." Then I thought about the day he told me that my jeans and tee shirt would suffice for my husband's funeral. At that very moment, I realized that the car he chose was no accident, but it was another blatant form of disrespect for Hicks.

Everyone was in their perspective cars, and it was time to head to the church. The church was less than five minutes away, but Hicks's uncle turned the drive in to almost a 30 minute one. He drove the route as slow as he could. I don't think any of us were able to go faster than two miles per hour. He drove so slowly that even Hicks's mom and sisters started to complain. The funeral home director could have led us to the church; especially since he had performed so many other funerals for the family. I couldn't understand why his uncle felt that this was his duty instead of just getting in another family car, or in line behind the procession. It seemed to me as if he wanted to be seen, and this procession was his own selfish parade that he was gloating in. He was like the Pied Piper, and we were all allowing him to lead us with his instrument; the ugly brown Lincoln.

When we finally made it to the church, it was packed with people. When I saw all the cars and the people outside, it made my heart leap in fear. I was so weak and nervous when I got out of the car, I could barely stand up. I scanned the church's parking lot, and I thought for sure I'd see some of my family waiting for me on the outside, but they were already seated inside the church. I knew I would have to make the walk alone, and my knees trembled under the thought of it all. I had just gotten use to my title of wife but would now have to wear a newer more painful title of widow. This new title also came with being thrown in to the spotlight; a spotlight that I had spent much of my life avoiding. I nervously walked through the sea of people and searched for a familiar face. When I did, I only saw strangers staring solemnly back at me. I dropped my head and proceeded to the church doors. When the doors opened, the church was full of people sitting and standing against the walls. As I entered,

I felt as if everyone's eyes were on me, and it made me feel very uncomfortable. I looked straight ahead and walked weakly towards the casket. The walk was like walking in sand with no oxygen, and when I got to the casket, I felt like I was about to faint. I ended up having to place both of my hands on the casket to balance myself so I wouldn't fall. It felt as if all my muscles and tendons were removed, and they were slowly being replaced with cement.

I closed my eyes and took a deep breath, and reluctantly looked down in to the casket. I saw the young man that once had so much life, and I thought about how it was taken from him. Hicks's skin had darkened a little more, but he still looked the same as he did on the night of the wake. I stood staring down into his face, and then reached over to touch him once more, and for the last time. That's when my hand was grabbed. I looked at the hand touching mine, and then turned to see who it belonged to. It was the funeral home director again, and he was wagging his head at me and telling me no. He also had his other hand on my back, and he was trying to nudge me on past the casket and to my seat. When he did this, I felt rage within me. I snatched away from his touch then stared meanly at him. I saw him nervously looking around to see if anyone had noticed while I continued to give him my death stare. I wanted everyone to see my behavior because I disliked the director greatly and had not forgotten all the things, I had stored in my memory about him. I hadn't forgotten about the crane my mom said she'd saw at his funeral home, nor had I forgotten about his jolliness, and later poor treatment the day we came to select the casket for Hicks. I hated the fact that he even had my husband's body and was going to profit from his burial. But most of all, I hated his touch, and I could sense that he was evil. Even though he had on white gloves, his touch disgusted me and made me feel nauseous. After feeling the nauseating waves going through my body, the director quickly removed his hands as if he felt something too. He then stepped away from me, and he stood with his hands folded in front of him with his head lowered. He wouldn't even look at me anymore, but now patiently waited for me to decide what I wanted to do. I stared at the director a little longer before turning my gaze back to Hicks. I took another visual picture of him, so that I could further store his face to my memory. I then kissed my fingers and touched his lips with them. I felt the cool fullness of his lips under my touch. I whispered and told him that I'd always love him, and then I left his casket and walked to my seat.

Once I was in my seat, my daughter was brought to me, and I watched as Hicks's family made their way up the aisle to view his body. They were devastated. His mom broke down crying and was quickly ushered to her seat. When his sister, the one who lived in our house approached Hicks's body, she let out a scream then leaned down in his casket and tried to hug him. The ushers stopped her, and she was then escorted away weeping. His other two sisters approached the casket and looked in at him, and then took their seats and sobbed. Hicks's cousin who had refused the medicine walked up to the casket next. When she looked in to the casket at him, she let out a blood curdling scream then fainted. She was then physically carried out of the church. The screams and cries frightened my daughter, so she began to cry too. My young aunt that sent my prom attire heard my daughter's cries, so she came and confiscated her from me. However, an usher soon brought her back when her cries became even greater, and it was because my daughter had never seen or met her great aunt before, so she was a stranger to her. The sermon and eulogy were a blur to me, but I remember all the beautiful music and comforting songs that were song. It was finally time to bring the funeral to a close, and I watched as Hicks's casket was closed, centered, then rolled down the aisle covered in white flowers. When the casket made it to the back of the church, I heard the crowd erupt in screams, and there was crying and moaning. As I listened, it sounded much like a sad choir in the wrong key.

The funeral was ending, so an usher came and stood near our pew. He asked us to rise, and then escorted our row of family members to the door. When my daughter and I reached the outside, I saw the tail end of Hicks's casket sliding into the hearse, and two ushers closed the doors. After the doors were closed, I saw Hicks's flower covered casket peeping out the window from behind two white accordion curtains. How I wished that it was all a terrible nightmare that I'd wake up from. I then watched as the hearse pulled away and headed towards the church's burial site which was just a few blocks away; still in viewing distance. The remaining ushers stayed on the church grounds, and they told the family that we would be joining the casket once the gravesite was set up. I felt sad and miserable. My husband was dead, my daughter was fatherless, and when I looked around at everyone; I saw people talking and laughing when my world was gone.

I continued to watch from the church as the hearse drove Hicks's casket to its final resting spot. I admired how beautiful the hill looked while they were placing his casket on the platform. One limo left the gravesite while the other stayed, and it headed back to the church. When it pulled up, the funeral director got out and called his other ushers over to him. They talked amongst themselves for a bit, and then the funeral home director came over to the crowd. He asked if he could have everyone's attention, and we all became silent in order to hear him. He told us that there was an issue with the grave, so the burial would be delayed. He said that it would take time to correct the issue and asked if we could return to the family home in the meantime. He never stated what the issue was, but it quickly circulated that the grave wasn't wide enough for the casket. How could a mistake like this happen when they'd buried so many people? Was this truly incompetence or was this no accident? I was dishearten and upset, and in disbelief. Anger and tears scorched my throat, and I wanted to scream. I saw my parents and others watching my behavior, but I didn't know what to do. What could I do?

As Hicks's family loaded in to limos and their perspective cars preparing for their journey home; my daughter and I got in the car with my family instead. I didn't want to go to the family house. I just wanted to go home. After we piled in to the car, my dad started it, and we headed out of the church's parking lot. He turned left on to the narrow road that led up to the main highway. The narrow road had a stop sign at the end of it, and when my dad got to it, he stopped and sat there. Across the highway we could clearly see the grave yard, and when we did, we saw Hicks's flower draped casket. It was still being guarded by the two ushers left there. When I saw this, my tears turned in to sobs, and my family sobbed along with me. Even my daughter cried because she saw all of us crying. As we sat at the stop sign weeping, I couldn't help thinking about how Hicks had died and left me, and I thought about how he too would be all alone. I would never see him again, and his young body would never age or grow old. My husband would be forever young, and his young body would lie for an eternity confined to a hole in the ground. Every scenario that I played out in my head was terrible when I thought about Hicks and his present state. However, my biggest disappointment would come later when I was unable to see him being physically placed in his final resting place.

When we arrived home, a few people showed up, but most of the funeral attendees went to Hicks's mom's home. When I got in the house, I went straight to my bedroom, laid across the bed, and balled my eyes out. I told myself that I wasn't going to cry anymore, but I couldn't help thinking about Hicks and how his casket had been left sitting on the hill, and it didn't sit well with me. I even found myself wondering if he'd be buried at all. I questioned his actual burial because I had spoken to his mom a day before his funeral, and she told me his insurance still had not paid out. I was wondering how she paid for everything, and if she didn't pay it, who did?

When Hicks and I married, he and I discussed changing his insurance policy. He told me that he was going to add me and our daughter as his beneficiaries, but he never got the chance to since his life was cut short. I don't blame him because in all honesty; what twenty-two-year-old think they're going to die? Hicks had an accidental death policy at his job, but when he died everything went to his mom since he never got the chance to change it. When his mom received the money, or how much she received was never disclosed or shared with my daughter and me. When I asked about it, she constantly told me that she had not gotten a thing, but she would let me know when she did. I would later find out that what she was telling me was not true. I finally checked it out with our employer, and they told me that the money had been disbursed, but they would not give me the date or the amount. I couldn't believe that she would lie to me, but I had the proof that she had, and it upset me even more. I would later learn about another insurance policy that Hicks was in, but this time, it would be one that his mom wouldn't want to accept.

One day, while I was out and about, I ran into one of Hicks's cousins. She told me that she had something to tell me, so we found a private corner in a store. She told me that she was at the house shortly after Hicks funeral when her aunt, Hicks's mom; got a visit from the funeral home director, a police officer, and Hicks's uncle's attorney. The trio asked Hicks's mom, if she'd come with them to Hicks's uncle's attorney's office to sign for her son's insurance policy. Hicks's mom questioned them, and she asked where had the policy come from because she wasn't aware of any other. They wouldn't answer her questions, but they went in to a song and dance about how the money was left for her granddaughter. They told Hicks's mom that it was a lot of money, and how it would make her granddaughter a "rich little girl." Hicks's mom wouldn't go with them, and she told them that she wouldn't be signing anything. Hicks's cousin then told me that when Hicks's uncle apparently got wind of what happened, he showed up to the house angry, and asked to speak to her aunt privately. She said they went in a back room, and she could hear voices raised but couldn't make out what was being said. She said she did however hear her aunt saying, "My son, my son" over and over and was weeping. She said that the next thing she heard was the uncle literally trying to force his sister to come with him, but when he tried another uncle intervene by pulling a gun on him. She told me that the uncle was then made to leave the house, and he did. When she told me this, chills went all over my body and I couldn't believe what I was hearing. She and I discussed how it was blood money that he was trying to collect, and if Hicks's mom would have gone with them, and accepted the money; who knows what may have happened to her.

Since she wouldn't sign, no-one involved with my husband's death could get their money. I wonder even to this very day, if the funeral home director ever did. If he didn't, I wonder what state that would have left my husband's body in? Is he even in the casket that he was in during his funeral, or in the plot that I saw his casket sitting near? I am questioning things because the day after his funeral, I heard rumors from people in the community saying that they saw Hicks's casket still sitting on the hill unburied several hours after his funeral. They also said that it was almost dark when they saw men finally filling in the grave with dirt. Hearing everyone's comments bothered me, so the next day, I asked my dad if he'd go with me to the grave. My dad told me to let everything go because it would only upset me further. He told me that going there would change nothing, but it would only make things even harder on me. I could have gone by myself, but I was scared. Plus, Hicks didn't have a headstone yet, and there were so many fresh graves that I probably wouldn't even have known which one belonged to him, so I didn't go.

Since Hicks's death, I have often contemplated having him exhumed. I want to finally know for sure if he's actually in a casket and buried there. Once I get this mental closure, I'll go from there forensically. In the back of my mind, I still feel as if he's not peacefully resting, so I guess I want to know if at least he has a final resting place. If I attempt to exhume him and find out that he's not there, at least I would have uncovered a major piece of the many grave secrets associated with his death.

10.

TATTLETALES

ALTHOUGH MY HUSBAND'S LIFE HAD ENDED, talk in the small community had not. One day, I went to get gas and was told by an associate that I should talk to the young gas attendant on duty. Knowing I'd already spoken to him once before when Hicks was missing, I asked them why. They said that the attendant told several people that the person he once believed was Hicks getting gas that day was not. He claimed that he later realized that it was his cousin who looked like him and was driving his car. The associate left my car then quickly got back in to theirs and drove away. I sat in the car and watched the young attendant from my review mirror. I sat there about five minutes thinking about what I would say to him to break the ice, and then what questions I would ask. Finally, I got out of my car and went over to him. As I walked towards him, I could tell he already knew why I was approaching and tried to act busy. He was sweeping, and just as I got to him, he turned his back to me and pretended that he didn't hear me when I called his name. I got closer and greeted him. He turned around and greeted me back, and I saw his eyes flickering from me to the cars that were passing by and coming in to the station. I could tell that he was nervous and scared. I immediately told him what I had heard and asked if he'd tell me if it was true. He scanned the station again then said, "Look, I don't want to talk about it nor be involved." I didn't pressure him because I could tell that he was afraid. He apologized and told me that he was sorry, and then he walked away. He wasn't the only one who was afraid, a lot of people in the community were; including me. Even though the young attendant didn't say a word, his behavior told me everything I needed to know at the time. I now knew that Hicks's cousin had indeed lied to me and my mom that day when he claimed he had not seen Hicks. This small piece of the puzzle further helped me know that Hicks death was no accident but was thought out and planned. When I got back to the car, I sat pondering what my next move would be. I knew if the young attendant knew something, so did others. I would just need to keep my eyes and ears open, so I could find out who all were involved, and who I would need to watch out for.

As time went on, more and more people continued to talk and share bits and pieces of what they knew. Although they were scared, they cared enough about Hicks to come to me and tell me what they had heard or knew. What was most surprising, I seemed to be getting more clues and information than the police; who apparently wasn't even looking into my husband's death anymore. One night, while visiting a friend's house that was a local bootlegger, I would get even more valuable information from a man that was supposed to be one of Hicks's friends. It was a Saturday night, and my mom and I decided to go get us a couple of drinks to unwind. We got there around eight thirty p.m., and took a seat near the door, and watched the coming and going of different people. We were there for about thirty minutes, when a friend of Hicks came over to us, and said he needed to talk to us because he had something, he wanted to get off his chest. We asked him to go ahead and tell us, but he told us he didn't feel comfortable telling us there. We asked what he meant by his statement. He then said, "I want to tell you, but we need to leave first because it's not safe for me to be seen talking to y'all." After Hicks's friend said this, my mom and I looked at each other then looked back at him. We watched as he stood nervously before us surveying the room. We kept trying to pry the information from him, and thought if we whispered our questions, it would make him feel comfortable enough to talk. This didn't work, and with each entering patron, he became more and more nervous. He'd started taking steps backwards away from our sitting area, in order to look as if he wasn't speaking to us. I became impatient and demanded that he tell us whatever he had to tell. I told him that we were planning to leave at nine thirty, so we needed him to hurry up, so we could go home.

My mom interrupted during my commentary, and she told Hicks's friend that we would leave and go somewhere else to talk with him. When she said this, I looked at my mom as if she were crazy and had lost her mind. I didn't trust anyone after what happened to my husband; especially one of his so-called friends. When my mom offered to go elsewhere; he said, "Yes, let's leave here and we can talk." I said, "No, we are not going anywhere with you, so if you can't tell us here, you can just keep what you claim you know." Hicks's friend's eyes looked shocked by my statement, but sad at the same time. He knew I didn't trust him. Hicks's friend looked around, and then came as close as he could to us, and then insisted that we leave with him. His insistence became pleas. He told us he really needed us to hear what he had to say, so he could clear his conscious because Hicks death had been eating away at him. Of course, my mom wasn't afraid and wanted to go with him, but I was, so I tried to convince her not to. I tried to tell her that I didn't want to hear what he had to say and told her that I believed that Hicks's friend was trying to set us up. My mom told me to stay calm and not to worry. She then whispered in my ear that if he tried anything, she would blow his head off. We both had our guns that night, but I knew if we were ambushed, it would take more than two guns. Hicks's friend watched us as we whispered, and I saw that he was now even closer to the front door. He looked nervous, but I didn't know if it was an act. If it was, I told myself that he was going to be my first casualty.

Hicks's friend finally made his way to the front door, and we watched as he walked out of it. We continue to sit there and talk for a few minutes; just in case someone was indeed watching. We said goodbye to our bootlegging friend and exited the house. When we got outside and was standing on the porch, Hicks's friend was waiting in his car, and tried to call us over to get in. As we left the porch, my mom yelled back at him, and told him that we would be taking hers instead. She opened her driver's side door and slid under the wheel. I walked around to the other side, opened the back door, and got in behind the passenger's seat. Hicks's friend watched us from his car, and he waited until he was sure no one was leaving or coming before he exited it. When he got out of his car, he quickly ran over to ours and got in. Once in, he lowered himself so no one could see him. I did the same because I was in the back seat, and I knew it would look strange if someone saw my mom chauffeuring me. When we pulled out of the driveway, Hicks's friend navigated us to a location he said was secure. I was scared out of my mind. I didn't like the fact that he'd be the one directing us, and it would be to a place he claimed would be private. The place he chose was a very secluded place in our small town, and it was on a high hill. Before we parked, I asked my mom to leave the car running; just in case we had to leave the scene in haste. Hicks's friend seemed anxious; even though we were supposed to have been the only ones there. He nervously looked around and search the darkness, and his behavior bothered me. I didn't know if he was expecting someone, or if he was simply making sure that we had not been followed. When he grabbed his chest and exhaled, I saw that he was indeed afraid. I now felt that he was getting ready to tell something he knew that he wasn't supposed to tell. From his wide eyes and twitching lips, I also believed that he knew the consequences of telling it.

My mom turned the car around and faced it towards the entrance of the road we had driven up. She then placed the car in park but left the engine running. I slid to the very middle of the back seat and faced Hicks's friend. He sat partially turned so he could see the both of us. When he saw that we were waiting for him to start, he searched the darkness one last time then said, "I could have told y'all where Hicks was all the time ya'll was looking for him, but I was too afraid." He was waiting for us to respond, but we didn't and continued to stare blankly at him. After he didn't get a response from us, he continued and said, "Hicks's dead body was lying behind New Elem Baptist Church the whole time, and it was later placed inside the basement of that church." He paused, and then appeared to be choosing his next words carefully before he said, "The body had been moved early that Sunday morning, so it wouldn't be discovered during church hours." We listened as he detailed how the body was moved and placed before it was time for its discovery. I then stopped him and asked, "Where was the body moved after it left the church basement, and who moved it?" He claimed that he didn't know. He was getting ready to resume his story when I stopped him again and asked, "How do you know so much if you weren't involved?" He looked back at me and searched my eyes in the darkness and said, "The Reverend asked for my help." He told us that the "Reverend" brought him to the very location we were in, and he told him his plan for Hicks. Hairs stood up on the back of my neck when I heard his words. I couldn't believe that we were now sitting in the same location where my husband's murder was planned. Why would he bring us to the actual spot if it was not a set up? My mom must have felt the same because after his statement, she pulled her gun and pointed it at his face. She cocked the trigger then told him that if he was trying to get us killed; he would be the first to die. The gun was unexpected, and it scared him so much that he immediately began to beg my mom for his life. He told my mom through pleas and tears how he was only trying to help us. He turned to me and said, "Hicks was my friend, I cared about him." He said that Hicks was just a boy under him and had never done anything to hurt him or anyone that he knew of. My mom didn't flinch; she kept her gun pointed at his face then told him to finish his story. I was in the back seat shaking, and I didn't want to hear any more of it. His words had frightened me so bad that I had practically started begging my mom to leave the secluded hill. I had experienced a similar situation like this before, and I didn't want to go through it again. My mom let out a loud yell; telling me to shut up and calm down. Her yell shocked but calmed me. I then sat quietly listening to my pulse race.

Hicks's friend nervously resumed, but now had his palms slightly up facing my mom's pointed gun. He looked like a man giving up when he was only giving up information. I grabbed the window roller and cracked my window, so I would be able to hear if there was any movement in the distance. Hicks's terrified friend reiterated that the "Reverend" asked him to meet him at our current place, and when he did, he was there waiting on him. He said when he arrived, he got out of his car and got in with the "Reverend." He then said that once he was in, he was immediately asked if he wanted to make some money. He said that his answer was yes, but then asked what he'd have to do. He looked back at my mom and paused before saying, "That's when he told me he wanted me to kill Hicks for him." I interrupted and asked, "Why would he ask you?" Hicks's friend responded, "He knew I was Hicks's friend, and that Hicks wouldn't be suspicious of me." I was furious, but I asked him why he sat and listened to Hicks's uncle. He responded, "What choice did I have, and I had to make him think I was considering it, so I wouldn't be killed myself." I yelled at him to continue his story because now my blood was boiling. He told us how he tried to pry the "Reverend" by asking what was it that Hicks had done, but he wouldn't answer. Hicks's friend then said, "I even asked why he didn't just do it himself." He said after that question, the "Reverend" told him that he was going to do it, but his plan had fallen through. The friend went on to say that the "Reverend" told him that his original plan was to kill Hicks and his brother. He said that he'd planned for them to die in a car accident while going to Birmingham, Alabama to pick up a car he'd promised Hicks. Once there, the breaks were supposed to have failed on Double Oak Mountain in Birmingham, and then Hicks and his brother would have died; either in a collision or a wreck.

Back in those days, several people had lost their lives going and coming on that mountainous road, and I guess Hicks's uncle knew this. Hicks's friend said that the "Reverend" told him that he'd planned for Hicks and his brother to drive a rigged car to a dealership in Birmingham, but they would wreck and die before they arrived. I knew that the friend wasn't lying because Hicks himself told me that his uncle had promise him a car, on the day he drove up in a new one. To this day, I believed that his uncle's plan also fell through because Hicks never learned to drive in Birmingham.

When I tuned back in from my thoughts, Hicks's friend was saying how the "Reverend" had retrieved some black gloves from under his seat, and then showed them to him. I interjected and said, "Wait a minute...some gloves?" He said, "Yes, gloves." "He said that the "Reverend" told him that he'd gotten them from "The Seven Sisters," and all he'd have to do was just put them on and touch Hicks, and the gloves would kill him instantly without leaving a mark. Hicks's friend said that he told the "Reverend" that he didn't know if he could do it. He said Hicks had never done anything to him, and he liked him. He said he also told the "Reverend" that he was having reservations because Hicks was married with a family, but he would think about it. Hicks's friend then said, "I know if I would have flat out said no, I would have never made it off that hill."

My mom and I sat shocked and speechless listening to his story. Suddenly, we heard sticks crackling as if something or someone was walking towards the car. I yelled out, "Something is out there!" My mom heard it too, and she didn't wait around to see what or who it was. She quickly put the car in drive, and she sped away down the hill as fast as she could. As we were leaving the hill, we were all looking back to see if anyone was coming behind us. Hicks's friend was yelling and telling my mom to hurry and get us off that road. I could tell that he was just as terrified as we were, and that's when I knew I could trust a large part of his story; even though most of it seemed unbelievable. If he had indeed lied, I knew that the promised new car was not one of them. As we road in silence while the car navigated the road, I thought to myself, "Well, Hicks's uncle made good on his promise, and Hicks was found dead in it."

We were almost back to Hicks's friend's car when I broke the silence. I asked him why he didn't tell Hicks what was about to happen to him, nor go to the police and tell what he knew. He said, "I didn't want to have nothing to do with it." I then leaned over the seat and told him how he was just as responsible for my husband's death as the people who did it. I screamed, "You knew what was going to happen, yet you didn't warn him!" I then screamed in to his ear and called him a murderer. The more I screamed at him, the lower he hung his head. I then said, "Hicks is dead right now because you didn't want to get involved, and you call yourself his friend!" I yelled at him and told him that he let my young husband meet an untimely and possible painful death. I also told him how our daughter would now have to grow up without her dad, and that his silence had destroyed our family and ruined my life. I was crying as I told him my feelings, but my tears were soon replaced with rage. I rambled through my purse then pulled my gun from it, and I held it in my hand. My mom slowed the car, and she searched for my face in the review mirror because she knew exactly what I was about to do. I could see her looking back at me in it, but I knew that she couldn't see me. She started calling my name as if I was a missing child, but I wouldn't answer her. My silence had both my mom and Hicks's friend worried. I saw him glancing over at my mom then back at the road because he was too afraid to look in to the back seat at me. I finally spoke and told him how bad I wanted to shoot him in the back of the head, and then throw his body from the car. I was contemplating it too, and I believe that my mom knew it and felt it.

My mom stopped the car in the middle of the road, and then began to beg me to calm down. She spoke in a low calm voice, and then told me how she didn't raise a murderer. She then tried to rationalize by telling me how hard it would be for me to live with myself, if I was responsible for someone losing their life; and used Hicks friend as her example. As she spoke, I listened, but never took my eyes off Hicks's friend. He was now breathing rapidly and staring at my mom, and his eyes were pleading with her to save him. They both waited quietly for my decision, and finally I told Hicks's friend that he wasn't even worth it. When my mom heard my words, she breathed a sigh of relief then agreed with me. When she resumed driving, Hicks's friend still couldn't relax because I continued to talk and threaten him the whole way to his car. He began to cry, and through his tears, he told me that if he could do things over again, he would do them differently. He was literally sobbing when he said, "I should have helped Hicks, and I'm sorry." I yelled, "It's too damn late for sorry, Hicks is dead now and it's your fault!" He laid his head in his hands and cried like a baby.

He was still sobbing when we got him back to his car. His car was the only one in the driveway when we pulled up, and there was a spotlight on it from the light pole. Seeing it, reminded me how Hicks's car looked the last night I saw it at the plant. Before he exited the car, he tried to turn and say something to me, but I pointed my gun in his face then told him to get out. He weakly opened the door while wiping tears. When he got out of the car, he walked towards it with his shoulders drooped and his head hung low. He came to us to clear his conscience and get things off his chest, but after I finished telling him how he contributed with his silence, an even heavier burden was placed firmly back on him. I could almost see the weight as he scampered back to his car. After that night, his life only got worse. A few months later he was shot and almost killed. After that, he had a massive heart attack and almost died again. Eventually, he died from cancer, and I heard that it was a long process, and he suffered greatly.

The next day was Sunday, and that night my mom and I went back to work. On our way, we discussed what Hicks's so-call friend told us. We contemplated how we should go and investigate the place where Hicks's friend said his body had been when it was missing. We decided to do it the following Monday morning after we got off work. I was scared like always, but my mom told me we wouldn't go alone this time. She said she would ask her brother to come with us. After we got off work, we drove to Equality, Alabama to pick him up. On our way, we saw Hicks's uncle beside the highway in a full suit and tie, and he was standing near his empty pulpwood truck looking at timber as we passed. When we got to my mom's brothers house, we went in and told him what we wanted with him. He was reluctant to come, and just like everyone else, said he didn't want to be involved. My mom wouldn't take no for an answer, and told him, "Boy, get your gun and come on!" My mom's brother didn't argue, he grabbed his gun and left with us. On the way down the road, Hicks's uncle was still there with his empty pulpwood truck standing in the same spot. I wondered why he was still there because he didn't have any wood on it, and as a matter of fact, I had never seen any wood on it. If he did indeed have timber, there wasn't anyone there to help him load it. Plus, I wondered how he planned to do any work at all in a full suit and tie. He dressed like this every day, and it looked ridiculous;

especially while in his truck and in the woods.

We drove on past him and stopped off at my parent's house to pick up my brother. When we got there and told him our plan, he grabbed a shotgun off my dad's rifle rack, and left with us. We drove towards the church where Hicks's so-call friend told us his body was held. When we got there, we drove to the side of the church, and noticed a path and followed it. The path led us to a pasture with a barn. Once we got in the pasture, ugly malnourished looking cows came from everywhere and surrounded the car. When I saw the cows, I then remembered a conversation Hicks and I had. He told me his uncle had a pasture with a lot of cows that nobody knew about. After he told me, I remember asking, how many cows did he have, and why was it a secret. Hicks replied, "A lot of them, my uncle is just rich, and folks are jealous of him."

Seeing the cows, made me think back to the small sickly-looking calf that was once tied to a tree in Hicks's uncle's yard, and I noticed how similar they looked. Now, we were amid a sickly-looking herd of them, and more were on their way. I guess they believed we were coming to feed them, and they looked as if they could have used several meals. More cows were leaping off a bank and heading for the car, and that's when I spotted a black bull on its way. It was in full speed as it leaped from the bank. Once it leaped, I looked down and saw an egg carton sitting on the bank. The carton was not a full egg carton, but it looked as if it had been cut in half to hold only four eggs. It looked very much out of place, so my mind immediately went to the voodoo I had heard rumored that Hicks's uncle was heavily involved in. At the time, I didn't believe in voodoo, but couldn't help thinking how the carton reminded me of the four of us in the car. Someone had to place it there, and since it was cows there and not chickens, I wanted to know what its purpose was.

I was no stranger to the name, "The Seven Sisters" because Hicks's so-call friend reference them the night he took us to the hill and discussed the gloves that supposedly came from them. I had also heard the name float throughout the community, and I heard stories of how Hicks's uncle was visiting them and gaining power from their help. I was now sitting in a car possibly looking at some of their work, and I became spooked. Something told me that it was time to leave, and when I expressed it, my family ignored me. My uncle and brother saw a barn in the distance and discussed going to look in it. I didn't like that idea at all, and I begged them not to leave the car. They told me to calm down because they had their guns and wasn't afraid. Then they asked my mom to drive them closer. The cows still surrounded us, so I asked my mom to honk her horn to see if it would scare them away. When she did, it made the cows scatter, but the bull didn't move; it continued to watch us. My mom drove the car to an area in the pasture and stopped. From our windows we could see several tire tracks and footprints, and they were leading to the barn. We all sat quietly looking at the prints, and then my mom turned to me and said, "This is where they killed him." I looked down across the pasture at the barn, and in my heart; I knew she was possibly right. I guess my brother and uncle also accepted my mom's statement because they no longer attempted to get out of the car. We all just sat there and quietly accepted what may have happened there.

We were at the pasture behind the church for less than fifteen minutes. When we drove back down the road, Hicks's uncle was at home. We all discussed how quickly he had gotten there; especially since we knew where he was originally. We took my brother home, and when he got out, he noticed that one of my mom's hubcaps was missing. We all questioned her, and she told us that she was sure that she had all of them before we went to the pasture. After hearing this I was worried, but my family didn't seem bothered. I couldn't help thinking how the hubcap would not only tell Hicks's uncle that someone went there, but it would also lead back to us. Although my family seemed unphased, I knew it wasn't a game because my young husband had just lost his life.

A few days later my fears came true, and my mom would personally get to see his reaction to her missing tire caps. She was sitting in her car at a local store waiting for one of my siblings to come out. Hicks's uncle pulled in driving his pulpwood truck, and just sat there. She said as he pulled in, she could see that he had on his signature three-piece suit with no wood on the back of his truck. She said that she turned and started rambling through her purse, but after a moment noticed that his engine never turned off. She said she looked back over to see what he was doing, and when she did; saw him sitting and staring at her. She told me that she stared back, and neither broke their stares or looked away. She said they were in a complete eye lock when he leaned over and glanced down at her tire with the missing tire cap, and then looked back up at her. My mom said after he did this, she immediately pulled her gun from her purse and sat it in her lap. She said she was nervous under his gaze, but knew she'd shoot him dead, if he got out of his truck and came over to her. My mom said they continued to stare at each other until finally he turned from her gaze and drove away. After the stare down with my mom, we never saw much of him after that. It was almost like he was avoiding us. My dad even commented on how he wasn't around much anymore, but we were all glad that he had made himself scarce.

Time passed, but I could still feel Hicks's presence. I could feel him everywhere. I would sometimes hear his car coming up the road towards my parent's house, but it would fade before it got there. My siblings even told me they often heard it too. Not only did Hicks's spirit linger with me and my family, but it lingered with others as well. People who had worked with him told me that his spirit still seemed to be among them at the plant. One day, one of Hicks's coworkers who he rode with each night to deliver yarn, came up to me. He told me that Hicks paid him a visit one night while on his regular route to deliver yarn. He said that he was getting ready to start his truck when his passenger side door opened. He said he waited to see who it was, but then felt something get in and sit down, and then the door closed. He told me that he immediately jumped from the truck, and he ran in to the plant and told everyone what happened. He told me that he had never experienced anything like that before, and wouldn't have believed it, if he had not witnessed it himself.

I've often heard that when a spirit lingers, it is because it is not at rest. I believe that Hicks is one of those spirits, and it's because of how he died. After all these years, he still come to me in dreams. He always asks that I not forget about him, nor let our daughter. I always promise that I won't. Now, not only must I keep his memory alive for our daughter, but I must also do it for our grandsons and future great grands that he'll never get to meet.

Hicks's life had ended, but that was not the end of Hicks's family's story. A few weeks after his death and burial, things would take a turn for the worse again. This time, the target would be his brother. One day, Hicks's brother up and vanished, and no one knew where he was. Just like Hicks, he lived in the family home, so when he didn't come home for a few days, it worried his mom. I was notified and told that the family was out in the community searching for him. Finally, the family received information that someone had seen him at a local store. They said that he was drunk and flagging down cars trying to get a ride home. They're family was then told that a white car stopped, and Hicks's brother was seen leaning in to it talking to the driver. After some time, they said that the back door opened, and he got in and they left with him. They said instead of heading towards Hicks's brother's home, it headed in the opposite direction.

A few days later, Hicks's brother showed up in the hospital. I got a call from the family saying that he was in intensive care fighting for his life. I borrowed my mom's car and went to the hospital. When I got there, his mother and siblings were all in the waiting room. When I entered, I walked over to Hicks's sister; the one who lived in our house. I asked her what happened, and she told me that the doctors said that her brother was poisoned, but he was expected to live. Hicks's mom sat quietly with her hands in her lap, and barely looked over at me. I knew she had a lot on her mind, so I didn't say anything to her. Suddenly, she started crying and said, "I done told him about drinking and taking drinks from people he don't know, and now look what happened." I turned back to Hicks's sister, and asked was he conscious. She said that they were notified that he was, and they were just getting ready to go to his room to see him. I asked if it was okay if I came with them, and they told me yes. When we got to the room, Hicks's brother was fully awake and alert. He seemed glad to see us. We asked him what happened, and he told us that he really couldn't remember. We asked him if he realized that he was in the hospital when he first woke up. He stared at us for a moment then said, "When I woke up, all I saw was uncle standing over me, and it scared me half to death." He then told us that he was so scared that it set off the heart monitor that he was connected to, and it caused the nurses and doctors to come running to his room. He also told us that when the nurses and doctors came in, and saw his uncle standing there; they asked how he had gotten in to the room, and then asked him to leave because he wasn't supposed to be there.

The family told him how long he'd been missing. Then they told him how it was said that he was picked up by someone in a white car. They then asked him if he knew who it was. I sat eagerly waiting to hear his reply; I wanted to know if it was the same car that had followed the family, and chased Hicks and I that morning. He sat there pondering their question, and then said that he didn't know. I watched as his family fussed at him, and they asked why he got in to a car with people he didn't know. They all told him that they believed that he was lying and continued to try to pry the information out of him. Hicks's brother went completely silent, and he would no longer speak to any of us about it. Someone had his tongue, and he wouldn't tell us who it was. It was a secret that he would also take to his grave because several years later, he would be found dead on the same highway as Hicks.

Hicks's big brother walked or hitched a ride wherever he went. It was never anywhere far, but usually up the road to someone's house or to a corner store. For as long as I can remember, he never had his own car, and it was mainly because he never held a job long enough to buy one. I remember how he would always hound Hicks about giving him a ride or letting him use one of his cars. Hicks would give him a ride, but he would never let him drive because he knew how he drank. One day, he stole one of Hicks's cars and wrecked it. I later watched their physical fight as Hicks beat him up for taking it. Hicks didn't beat him too bad because he knew that he was drunk, and I even watched Hicks pick him up and dust him off afterwards. Hicks's big brother was the quietest person you'd meet through the week when he wasn't drinking, but he'd let the dogs out when he got a smidge of alcohol in him, and his mouth would be non-stop. Just about everyone in our community knew how his brother was. Also, almost everyone knew that if he walked somewhere, he'd never walk far before he'd catch a ride. Knowing his behavior, is also why it surprised me when I got the news that he'd died while walking on Highway Number Nine.

It was reported that Hicks's big brother was run over multiple times by the cars that traveled on the highway. Based on how his body was lying in the road, people assumed that what they saw was an animal. Talk throughout the community circulated, and several people said they saw him drunk earlier that night. They also claimed that he was talking and reminiscing about his uncle and brother. Whatever he said must have gotten in to the wrong ears because it is ironic how he was found dead on the same highway as his little brother. No one was ever arrested, and it was ruled an accident. However, I have my suspicions, and believe that one of the persons that helped kill Hicks; also took part in killing his brother.

Although some of the goons were hired unknowns, I also believe that several of them were distant and close relatives that were looking for a payday. I'd even gotten word that one of Hicks's close cousins was involved. It got back to me that he was overheard saying, "Didn't nobody kill Hicks but his wife's family." This angered me deeply, but I also believe that I knew why he was saying it, and it was to take the focus off him. Hicks's cousin had always seemed jealous of him. While I was at the family's house, he would periodically drop in. He would never speak to me nor even acknowledge my presence, but I always noticed how he'd watch Hicks from the corners of his eyes. One day, I asked Hicks about him and their relationship. Hicks told me that he didn't believe that his cousin liked him, and he said that it had been that way since they were kids. Hicks told me that he believed that his cousin was jealous of him because of his light complexion. Hicks said that as kids, he'd try to get his older brother to exclude him from games. Hicks's brother was dark too, and Hicks said that they would be told by their cousin, "Don't let the white man play with us."

Shortly after Hicks went missing, his close cousin reappeared with his hand wrapped up in bandages. While visiting Hicks's family one day, I even overheard them talking about the hand injury, and they wondered how it happened since he would never say. I believed that I knew, and it was because I believed that he was a culprit in Hicks's murder. After the hand injury, I found myself constantly thinking about Hicks's cousin, and the possible role he played in the death. Eventually, my constant thoughts and anger led me to a plan of revenged.

One night, while at home, I became overwhelm with anger, sadness, and grief. It was about ten thirty; my mom was home, so I asked her if I could borrow her car. She said I could use it, but then asked where I was going so late. I told her that I just needed to get out of the house because I was going stir crazy, but I wouldn't be gone long. She asked if I wanted her to go with me, but I told her that I just wanted to be alone. She stared solemnly at me as I grabbed up the keys and headed to the car. When I got in, I sat there and cried. I cried because I was still missing my husband, and I wanted very badly to see him and talk to him but knew I couldn't. As I sat there, I felt like my heart was going to explode, but I went ahead and started the car because I knew my mom was listening for the car's engine. I backed out of the yard and drove to the end of the drive way. Once I got there, I sat there because I didn't know which direction to go. I had no plan, I just knew I had to get out of the house. Something came to me and said, "Go to your friend's house, and get a drink." I turned left and headed up the dusty road towards my bootlegging friend's house.

When I got there, he wasn't home, and no one was in his drive way. I sat up under the big spot light in his yard that once illuminated Hicks's friend's car, and I cried like a baby. I don't know how long I was there, but as soon as I was about to leave, another car pulled in. When I looked over at the driver, I saw that it was Hicks's close cousin. I quickly perked up and dried my tears. When he saw me, he waved, and when I waved back; he exited his car and walked towards mine. On his way, I thought to myself, "This is perfect, I am about to get him." When he got to my window, I slightly lowered it, smiled, and then asked what he'd been up to since the last time I saw him. He smiled back and told me that he hadn't been up to anything, and that he was coming to get a drink but saw that things were closed. I expressed the same sentiments. He then asked what I was about to do. I told him that I was going to go get gasoline to refuel my mom's car, and then asked him if he'd go with me. He said okay, and then jotted back over to his car and locked it, and then he returned and got in to mine. Once in, he asked what station I'd be going to because it was late. I told him that I was going to drive to the one in Semen because I knew that it was still opened. He said okay, and we headed there.

We weren't five minutes into the drive before Hicks's cousin looked over at me and said, "You know, I've always liked you and found you attractive." I said, "Really?" He then told me how he was kind of jealous when he first saw Hicks with me, and then told me how he wanted me for himself. I faked a smile and pretended to be listening to him, as he went on and on. He never noticed that I had increased my speed because he was too busy trying to flatter me with his words. As the car sailed down the road; his words were like white noise because I could only think about what I was going to do to him once I got him where I wanted him. We were almost in Semen when Hicks's cousin reached over and began to rub my thigh. I glanced over at him and gave him a wicked smile. When I exited the main highway, I turned on to a dirt road. I drove down the road a bit from the main highway. When I stopped the car; instead of reaching down to put it in park, I reached down in to my purse instead, and pulled my gun from it. I quickly turned on the car's interior light, and pointed my gun in to his face, and I saw his smile fade. Hicks's cousin immediately began to beg for his life. He never asked any questions as to why I was doing it, but only pleaded with me to spare him. I turned the car's high beam on and yelled at him to get out. He opened the door and quickly did as I instructed, and then turned back around to me with his palms up. I got out too, and then made him walk to the front of my car. When he stood directly in front of my car's high beam, I told him to get on his knees. When his knees touched the ground, I told him that I was about to shoot him in the back of his head. After I said this, he began to beg more, but I didn't feel any sympathy for him. I told Hicks's cousin how his comments about my family killing Hicks had gotten back to me, and that I was going to make him pay for what he'd said. He'd started to cry, so I yelled at him to shut up. I told Hicks's cousin how I believed that he'd help kill Hicks, and that I had planned to kill him, and that was why I had brought him there. He was sobbing and telling me how he wasn't involved. He then said, "I injured my hand working on a car." I responded and said, "Did I ask you about your hand?" He didn't answer my question; he only resumed his pleading. Then he said, "Hicks was my cousin, I wouldn't kill my own family, please believe me!" I then asked him, "If Hicks was your cousin, why would you try to mess with his wife?" He could only shrug his shoulders and shake his head while sobbing. I continued to watch the frighten man before me, and all I could hear was something screaming in my ear, "Kill him!" I was getting ready to squeeze the trigger when suddenly, my conscious seeped in and said, "You're not a killer, do you really want this man's blood on your hands?" "What about your daughter, and what happens if you get caught?" After the questions by the unknown voice in my head, I found myself shaking and sobbing right along with Hicks's cousin. I then yelled at him to get up, and when he did, he stood shaking under my pointed gun. I walked back to the car, and then told him to come get in. He came to his opened door and slid in with my gun still pointed towards him. I told him to close his door. After he closed the door, I warned him that if he tried anything, I'd shoot him, or possibly kill both of us while driving. As I spoke, he kept saying okay as if he was hypnotized by my voice. As I drove, I would quickly glance over at him, and I noticed that his palms remained up the entire time; all the way up the road.

That night, I drove faster than I'd ever driven before. When I got Hicks's cousin back to his car, I had to literally skid in to the yard because I was going so fast. When we got there, I yelled at him to get out. He looked as if he had just been in a war. His face was ashen, and streaked with dried tears, and his pants where wrinkled and dirty at the knees. He stiffly got out of the car, and before he could close the door, I took off towards home. Some weeks later, I saw Hicks's cousin at a traffic light, and he honked his horn at me. My window was down, and when I looked over at him, he said, "How you doing Ms. Dean?" I told him that I was fine, and I drove off when the light turned green. After that night on the vacant road, every time Hicks's cousin would see me, he'd greet me as "Miss Dean," and would then ask me how I was doing. I never held another conversation with him, and once I spoke, I would walk away.

After a long time of not seeing Hicks's cousin, I would finally see him for the last time. One day, out of nowhere, he walked up to me and asked for a hug. When I saw him, he looked feeble and weak, so I barely recognized him. I had been told that he was battling cancer, and I could clearly see that it had gotten the better of him, as he stood before me with his arms stretched waiting for my hug. It came to the tip of my tongue to tell him to get the hell away from me, but my daughter was there, so I didn't want to make a scene. I went ahead and gave him a slight hug. He died a few weeks later, but I knew that my hug was his way of asking for forgiveness for what he'd done. Since he knew he was dying, I guess he believed that my hug would somehow absolve him of his sin.

11.

Brown Eyed Girl

EVENTUALLY, EVERYTHING BECAME TOO MUCH for me and I left Alabama. I was tired of feeling alone, sad, and depressed. I was also very tired of feeling scared, so I took my daughter and moved to Philadelphia with my young aunt. I knew if I moved, I wouldn't have to feel bad about saying no to Hicks's mom when she wanted to keep our daughter. I couldn't bring myself to let my daughter stay with her while knowing that her brother was still lurking. She had done so little to get justice for her own son, so I knew it would possibly be the same if something happened to my daughter. Plus, I still had not forgotten how we were financially treated after his death. Hicks had been dead for a few months, and his mom seemed secretive and guarded when I talked about him. I recalled asking her if she had gotten his death certificate and if she could let me see it. She told me she had, but she would never show it to me. I could've just as easily gotten my own copy, but I guess I avoided it because it would then make Hicks's death real. My actual first copy of Hicks's death certificate was given to me by our daughter. She told me she purchased it because she had grown tired of me talking about how I wanted to see it. She also told me how she hoped it would give me some resolve. It didn't, and further opened old scar tissue.

I continued to express my anger about Hicks's death, but it seemed that I was the only one who continued to care about it. When I would try to discuss his life or death with his mom, she would tell me to let it go and let God handle it. I would even try to talk about fun memories of him with her, and she'd tell me that she didn't want to hear it, or even talk about him. I understood that it was painful for her because it was painful for me too, but her willingness to completely block out her son's memory; even the happy things, enraged me. Soon, even her presence bothered me, and not only did I not want to be around her, I didn't want my daughter around her either.

When my daughter and I got to Philadelphia, it was a good change of pace. It was very different from the south, and for a while, I was happy. However, as the days rolled on, Philly remained too big for me, and I grew homesick. I was accustomed to the quietness and darkness of the back woods. Although I enjoyed being there with my aunt and other family members, after two months I decided to leave. When my daughter and I left, we moved to Cocoa Florida with my sister and her husband. Florida felt almost like home, it was not as busy and had a country feel. After a few weeks there, I got a job at McDonnell Douglas as an assembly worker. I was responsible for assembling wires on bazookas and other military equipment. I loved my new job, but the racism I experienced on it made it difficult for me and other blacks. However, I maintained, and eventually I was able to move me and my daughter from my sister's house to our own place. It was a beautiful home. It was big and spacious, and we both loved it. It had a big beautiful back yard that was fenced in. I filled it with all sorts of toys for my daughter, and she spent most of her time outside playing with them. I had finally begun to get my footing at starting my life over. I still missed Hicks and thought about him every day; seeing his resemblance in our daughter made it hard not to. Not only did I miss Hicks, but I also missed my mom and younger siblings. I became homesick again, but I knew Florida was a good move for me and my daughter. I stayed and continue to reach out to my mom and siblings by telephone, and always promised to visit soon.

I was in Florida only ten months after the death of Hicks when I receive a shocking call from my mom. When I answered the phone she screamed, "He done did it again!" I stood holding the phone in total confusion while my mom rambled out words that I couldn't comprehend. She was talking so fast, so I yelled at her and asked her to slow down and repeat what she'd said again. When she did, I heard her say that another murder had taken place, and the victim was the girl. I was still confused and said, "What girl?" My mom then told me who the girl was, and it ended up being the niece of Hicks's uncle's third wife. The same young girl Hicks was often asked to pick up, the brown eyed girl I'd seen driving in to the gas station that day, and the same girl my brother said was his best friend with strange markings in her hands. I tuned back in from my thoughts, and heard my mom asking me if I was listening. I assured her that I was, and when she was sure that she had my full attention, she began to tell me how the young girl died.

When my mom started her story, I couldn't help but notice how it sounded as she was reading the beginning pages of a horror novel. She started by saying, "The night was dark, rainy, and dreary." This beginning was much like the beginning of all the other murders that had taken place in our small community. My mom said that she was on her way home from work when she saw a bunch of flashing lights from several police cars and an ambulance. As she got closer to the lights, several cops were directing traffic away from a car she assumed had wrecked. She said the whole place was lit up, and from a distance she could see legs sticking out from under the car. When she got in direct view, she saw a car with a missing wheel and a jack lying near it. My mom paused as if she was giving me a moment to breathe, and then said, "I didn't know who it was at the time, but I saw the axle of the car on top of the girl's face." I yelled out, "What!" My mom continued and said, "When I looked at the car itself, it belonged to Hicks's uncle." I screamed, "My God Momma!" My mom sadly spoke again and said, "Yes, he done killed that poor girl."

I stood there numbly holding the phone because I knew there'd be a made-up story to explain this death too. I started to feel nauseated, but I continued to listen as my mom gave a play by play account of what happened. She told me according to the story; the young girl supposedly had stolen Hicks's uncle's car, and after he noticed it missing, he called and notified the cops. However, while she was driving it, the tire blew out, so she got out and attempted to put on the spare. My mom paused then said, "I never heard of anyone getting under a car to change a tire, but that's how she was found." My mom went on to tell how the car fell on her face and crushed her skull. I asked if the police were buying the story, and my mom said, "I don't think so because the authorities have taken the car in to evidence." She then told me that when they examined the trunk, they found large amounts of saliva from the young girl's mouth. My mom then relayed how the community was in an uproar about the death. She told me how there were rumors that the girl was placed in a freezer, and frozen alive. She also told me how neighbors of Hicks's uncle even claimed to have seen him dragging something on a white sheet, and then placing it in the trunk of his car.

After hearing my mom's story, I became excited. Yes, my heart went out to the girl and her family, but I couldn't help thinking about how her death would help get justice for Hicks, and then for the other members of his family. His uncle would finally get what was coming to him for all the combined things he'd done. Hicks wasn't that much older, but the girl was a child, so I just knew that her death would be enough to finally get a conviction. My mom was in mid-sentence when I cut her off and asked, "Momma, what jail is he in?" To my surprise and disappointment, she sighed then responded, "Girl, he ain't even in jail." I screamed out, "What!" "What more does this bastard have to do?" Knowing that he was still free even after the girl's murder upset me, and so I began to cry. I felt as if justice had failed too many times, and to me it seemed a shame that no one in the community was even trying to stop him. My mom silently listened as I cried on the other end of the phone. The news that once had me happy and excited now turned my stomach sour. Hicks's uncle had gotten away with so much already, and now he was about to get away with killing the young girl. Maybe he did have someone or something protecting him after all, and it made me even sicker thinking about that possibility. I finally calmed down enough to ask when the funeral would be held, and my mom told me that week. Just like Hicks's funeral, it was going to be another speedy one. My mom then told me where it was going to be held. I noticed that it wouldn't be at a church, but at a funeral home instead. I was also surprised to learn that it wasn't going to be at the one used to prepare Hicks's body.

After my mom and I hung up, my tears reignited. I slid down

the wall and sat on the floor, and I thought about how Hicks was gone and now the brown eyed girl was too. I thought about how happy and full of life she looked the day I saw her pull in to the station and go in to the store. Now, just like Hicks, she was cut down in the prime of her life. I thought about how her head was crushed under the weight of the car, and I hoped that she hadn't suffered. I began to question God, and I asked Him why He was allowing the devil to reign. I then got on my knees and prayed that He would remove the monster out of our community and off the earth. After I finished praying, I got up and went to the door and stared out at my daughter playing with her toys. As I watched her play, in the back of my mind I thought, "If he'll kill a sixteen-year old girl, he'd have no problem murdering my daughter too." I opened the door, and then called my daughter to me. When she got to the screen door, I opened it, and then pulled her up in to my arms and hugged her. My daughter was all I had, but I still felt guilty for keeping the remaining part of Hicks from his mother. I knew they wanted to see each other, but I knew I had to keep my daughter safe from her not so great uncle.

It seemed as if the murders were never going to end because Hicks's uncle had gotten bolder with each kill. Now, instead of just taking out his family, he was starting to cross over and take the lives of others outside of it. I couldn't help thinking about his audacity to kill his wife's niece, and I wondered how she was taking it. Hicks's uncle was Satan on earth, and I hated him with every fiber of my being. Ever since Hicks's death, I'd fantasize about his final demise. Although I was in Florida, I would continue to play out the best scenario for him. Even if my mind placed him in jail, I sought out the death penalty for him. I even fantasized about what I'd wear to his funeral. I told myself I would wear raggedy blue jeans and an old faded tee shirt. It was almost the same outfit that he'd once found appropriate for my husband and his funeral. I also planned how I would spit in his face while he lay in his casket, and I told myself that I wouldn't even care if someone was watching. While venting to my mom after Hicks died, I told her my intentions for his uncle. She never said a word, she just stared at me with eyes that were absent of enthusiasm. Little did she know, I meant every word!

12.

KARMA

It was a beautiful sunny Florida day, and I was outside playing in the yard with my daughter when I heard my phone ringing. I ignored it and it stopped, but immediately it started ringing again. I told my daughter that we had to go in, but she didn't want to. I persuaded her by telling her that we would race, and then she took off. As we entered the house the phone stopped ringing, but immediately sprung to life again for the third time. At that point, I knew that it was a very important call, and I hoped that my family was okay. My daughter got to the phone first, and when she removed it from the receiver, she passed it to me. When I said hello, it was my young aunt, and she screamed in to my ear, "The preacher is dead, come home!" When I heard this, my heart almost leaped out of my chest. I made her repeat her statement because my mind couldn't process what she had just said, and I thought I heard her incorrectly. When she repeated her words again, I let out a big scream and said, "Thank you God!" My scream scared my daughter, and she stood staring at me as if I were crazy. I told my aunt that I needed a moment. I sat down the phone and scooped my daughter into my arms and took a seat on the floor. My daughter was still staring at me with worry, but when I smiled and kissed her, she left my arms and found a toy on the floor to play with.

When I picked back up the phone, I told my aunt that I was ready to hear what she had to say. My aunt began by telling me that she was currently at home from Philadelphia visiting her mom. She said the two of them were in the kitchen when her mom got a call. The caller told her that there had been a shooting at the funeral home, and one person was dead. The caller didn't have all the details but said that the killer fled the scene after the shooting. After the conversation ended, my aunt said my grandmother immediately received another call. This caller was at the young girl's funeral when the shooting took place. They told my grandmother that the Reverend was shot and killed while sitting on the second pew in the family section. They said a man jumped up on to the first pew, and then fired several rounds at point blank range in to the Reverend's head. They said right before the incident, a family member cried out, "You done killed our baby, and we're gonna get you!" Then they saw and heard shots from the man's gun, and then watched as the preacher's head fell backwards with blood pouring from it. The caller told how everyone leaped from their seats and rushed the exits; even trampling over one another as they went.

I found myself grinning from ear to ear as she told me what happened. I thought to myself, "I hope you felt every bullet and every bit of pain you bastard!" My aunt said that the community was in an uproar about the assassination, and everyone had different accounts of what happened. She told me however; one stood out to her, and it came from an usher attending to the funeral. She told me he remained in the funeral home with the preacher's body after the shooting, and he said that his blood and brains sounded like a heavy rainstorm as it poured from his skull to the carpet. The more I heard about Hicks's uncle's demise the more I wanted to hear. This was the best news that I could have ever hoped or prayed for. Was he really and finally dead? I never thought the death of someone could bring me so much happiness, and I felt almost as if I needed to pinch myself to make sure that I wasn't dreaming. I had killed this man so many times in my mind, and now he was finally dead. I was still in La-La Land when my aunt said, "You and the baby can come home now, you'll be safe." Hearing those words made my heart leap for joy. I would now be able to see my family, and my daughter would be able to see hers.

That night, I could barely sleep. I tossed and turned in my bed, and I replayed what my aunt and mom told me over and over in my head. I stayed up well in to the morning planning my trip to Alabama, and my funeral wardrobe. You would have thought I had won the lottery I was so happy. I thanked God for hearing my prayer, and then talked to Hicks in my head. I told him that he could now get some type of peace knowing that his uncle was in hell. I even talked to Hicks's other family members who had lost their lives to the preacher. I was on cloud nine celebrating the death of someone who I believed was pure evil, and I could hardly wait to see him flat on his back. However, fate would have a different plan for me, and to this day when I think about what happened, it is still one of my greatest disappointments.

A few days before the scheduled funeral, my brother in-law told me that he would drive me to Alabama. He then came back a day before and said that he couldn't take off work until the day of. Once he told me this, I called the airlines, and schedule a flight for me and my daughter. When I told my sister my plans, she begged me to wait until the day of the funeral, so we could all travel together. She said we would leave out early that morning in order to make it there on time. I said okay and cancelled my flight. The day of the funeral, the plans fell through. I was up before day, packed, and ready to go, but my sister and her husband didn't show. Every time I called her, she said that they were on their way. When they finally arrived, it was so late that we couldn't have made it to Alabama in time, if we'd taken a jet. I was so angry at her that I cried. Thinking back, I believe that my sister intentionally compromised my trip. Also, I believe that she planned and colluded with my mom to foil it. However, my mom was probably the real culprit, and used my sister to prevent me from going to the funeral and making a fool of myself. It was my own fault for telling my mom my plans for Hicks's uncle. I guess her once unenthusiastic look turned out to be a look of belief. My mom knew if I said something, I usually meant it, and would act on it; especially if I was angry.

When we finally made it to Alabama and got to my mom's house; friends and family bombarded me. They all wanted to tell me about the preacher's death as if I didn't know. Plus, they all had different stories on what happened to the girl, and if they didn't know it; they claimed that they knew someone who did. As I listened to the chatter, I thought to myself, "Now, they want to talk, but when Hicks died; they didn't want to be involved." I guess things are different when the Community Boogie Man dies. However, I noticed that several of them still seemed afraid. When I questioned them on why they were afraid, I was told that they believed that the preacher was going to return from the dead, and they said that "The Seven Sisters" were going to bring him back. There were even claims that the Sisters showed up to his funeral in a black limousine but wouldn't get out. What I found most ridiculous is that they claimed they had gone and purchased guns in case he did come back, and never thought once about the impossibility of killing something that had already died once. The rumor mill was incredibly large, but I only focused on realistic information. One day, I spoke with one of Hicks's uncle's neighbors, and I was told that after his death; his third wife created a large bonfire in their front yard. He said he and several neighbors watched as she burned items from inside the house, and they believed she was burning evidence.

I learned early in life that you need to be careful who you call friend, and I've taught my daughter this. I lost a husband because his so call friend didn't feel the need to warn him that he was going to be set up and killed, so today I have a strong distaste for even the word. The third wife made this mistake too with several of her trusted friends. She called on them to help her clean her deceased husbands house, and together they burn and destroyed items. However, the third wife's friends were no different than any other friend because they quickly betrayed her trust. They went throughout the community telling what they'd seen in the house while there, also what they destroyed. They claimed they saw cat guts in jars, and several hypodermic needles above door frames. I knew many of the stories were fabricated, but there was one I believed, and I got to see her proof with my own eyes.

One of the trusted friends ended up being a family member who was married in to Hicks's family. While there helping the third wife clean, she secretly confiscated insurance policies she'd seen lying around, and took them home. When she got there, she called a few family members to her house to show what she'd confiscated without the preacher's third wife knowing. She was informed that I was home, and so I was called to the house as well. Once there, I got a chance to witness the look on everyone's face when they picked up policies with their names on it. The policies were all dated, and one of Hicks's cousins was in disbelief when he saw his policy in his wife's hand. She read his name on the policy out loud, and then she showed him the future date on it that was not so distant. When I saw him reviewing it, he looked as if all life was draining out of him. He then grabbed it from her hand and left the room. He was gone for quite a while, but when he returned; he looked relieved. I'm sure it was because he knew that he wouldn't have to face what Hicks and all the others faced; since his uncle was now dead. He returned to the table and silently watched as his family continued to discuss the policies laid out before them. As I sat there watching each of their faces, I couldn't help but to think about Hicks. I bet he had a pre-dated policy too, and the difference between he and his family sitting before me was that his uncle got a chance to make good on it.

After being there a while, I arose and apologized for having to leave, but told them that since I had just gotten back in town; there were still more people I needed to see. When I left the house, they were still discussing their policies, and were questioning why their deceased son, brother, and uncle had them. I left and immediately went back to my parent's house and told them what happened. After I told them, they wagged their heads and expressed how it was a crying shame that Hicks and all the others were killed for money, and nothing was done about it because people were getting paid off. We then talked about how glad we all were that the man behind it all, was finally dead.

A few days later, a family friend that worked at the funeral home where Hicks's uncle was shot and his body prepared, came to visit. When he saw that I was there, he asked to speak to me alone, so we went outside and sat on the steps of the porch. He looked over at me with sympathy in his eyes then said, "I'm so sorry about what happened to your husband and little girl's father." I thanked him and fought back tears. He then said to me, "I know you've probably heard stories about how the Preacher is not really dead, but I'm hear to tell you that he is." He then said, "You don't ever have to be afraid because I split his head open myself and removed the bullets from it." I already knew that Hicks's uncle was indeed dead, but an invisible weight was lifted with his words. The family friend then told me the condition of Hicks's uncle's body before he prepared it. He said that when he removed his clothing, his body and underclothes were filthy. He said that he couldn't believe that a man who walked around in a three-piece suit and tie every day could be that filthy underneath his garments. We finished our conversation with him reassuring me again that the preacher was indeed dead, and that I was safe despite the stories even he had heard circulating about "The Seven Sisters."

After the death of Hicks's uncle, the habitual deaths in their family stopped, but the rumors never did. Forty plus years later, if Hicks's uncle's name is mentioned; people will stop in their tracks to listen or tell what they know or have heard about his murders. People are still so intrigued, that when a local newspaper in Alexander, City run its anniversary edition about him, it sells out. However, it's usually only old recycled information with a few added lies to enhance the story. The writer was a local liar who claimed that he once interviewed me and Hicks's mom to get some of his information. I had never met or spoken to him ever, nor have I ever even shared my story with anyone until now.

There is still a stigma left behind in my small community

because of what happened back in the seventies with the preacher and his victims. However, for the younger generation living there; it seems more like an urban legend or ghost story, but the things that happened were real. It is sad that no one in Hicks's family were ever brave enough to stand up boldly and address what happened; including me until now. In fact, no-one connected to the murders never even addressed how they felt; except the preacher's killer, who years later proudly told the local newspaper that he killed the preacher to avenge his loved one; the young girl. His bravery showed me that after years of sitting on my silence and pain, and not wanting to hurt Hicks's family; including my daughter, I also needed to be brave. It was a hard decision that I contemplated because I know my truth will hurt and open old wounds, and possibly create new ones. However, I felt that it was time I told my story because not only had it gone too many years untold, but I realized that I would not be able to totally heal until I did.

13.

SEEKING CLOSURE

MANY WILL ASK, why didn't she use specific names in her book? My answer to this question is; when you give evil a name, you give it power, so I purposely left it nameless. In time, I believe God will reveal all, so I'm going to continue to watch and pray that I don't fall in to temptation; because I still have so much pent-up anger about my husband's death. When I think about him, I think about how his life was stolen before he even got the chance to really live. I also think about his uncle, and the goons he hired to kill him, and how they also tried to kill me. The one goon that I think about most is Hicks's cousin; the one that lied to me and my mom that morning when we were looking for him, and the one the gas station attendant told others he'd seen driving Hicks's car when he was missing. I hope he doesn't believe that he's gotten away with things.

Believe it or not, this same cousin has even taunted me over the years. One night, I was at a club when he boldly approached me and said, "If you come and go with me, I'll tell you what happened to Hicks." After he said this, I was so shocked by his boldness that I ended up slapping his face as hard as I could. I couldn't believe that he was attempting to disrespect me like that. The slap shocked and angered him, and the sound of it ricocheted across the club, and drew attention to us. He was preparing to retaliate but was stopped by my uncle; who he didn't realize was present. My uncle came over and asked me what was going on. I told him what Hicks's cousin had said to me, and my uncle became enraged after he heard the words that spilled from my mouth. My uncle then said, "Wait right here!" Hicks's cousin frantically watched as my uncle disappeared behind the club's door, but quickly returned with a shot gun from his car. When patrons in the club saw my uncle re-enter with the gun; they screamed and sought cover. However, those who knew my uncle came over and pleaded with him to put the gun down. They tried to convince my uncle that Hicks's cousin wasn't worth going to jail over, and they begged my uncle to spare his life.

By some divine miracle, my dad entered through the club's doors. When he walked in, he immediately looked over and saw me, and rushed over when he saw his brother holding the gun. When my dad got to us, he saw the gun pointed at Hicks's cousin, and asked his brother what was going on. My uncle wouldn't look at my dad, nor did he respond, so my dad spoke in a calm voice and asked him to put the gun down so they could talk. My uncle slightly lowered it, but his finger remained on the trigger, and so did his eyes on Hicks's cousin. My dad tried to inquire about the incident, but we all stood silently. My uncle then looked Hicks's cousin squarely in the face and said, "Stay away from my niece or I will blow your head off!" Hicks's cousin quickly told my uncle that he would, and then tried to explain to my dad what happened. He said, "I wasn't trying to bother her, I just wanted her to talk to me like I see her talking to everyone else." He then told my dad that he didn't understand why I was ignoring him and treating him mean. My dad looked at him as if he wasn't buying his story then said, "If she doesn't want to talk to you, accept that, and leave her the hell alone."

Hicks's cousin was right when he said I was treating him differently, but he knew why. After Hicks died, I wouldn't speak to him nor even look in his direction. I can't stand him! That night in the club while he stood playing victim; with eyes darting from my dad to my uncle's gun; I had zero sympathy for him. Watching how afraid he was, I could only think about how afraid Hicks was during his last moments, so it satisfied me when I saw him fearing for his life. My uncle's eyes continued to flicker from Hicks's cousin and then back to me, and I knew exactly what my uncle was waiting on. But, just like the day at the funeral home with my dad and Hicks's uncle, and the night in the car with Hicks's fake friend, I couldn't bring myself to cause anyone's death, or be responsible for someone in my family going to jail. My mom was right, she didn't raise me to be a murderer, and I personally don't want anyone's blood on my hands.

That night, Hicks's cousin was spared one of his nine lives; since I asked my uncle not to shoot him. When my uncle let him go, he quickly scampered out of the club like the human rodent he is. After he left, my uncle's friends and other clubbers came over to us and told us how we'd made the right decision because he wasn't worth killing. To this day, he remains a sneaky, conniving, money hungry, and untrustworthy little man, and I still loathe him. Since he's always been pestilence for our small community, I was told after the incident to watch out for him due to his sneakiness. I responded and told those individuals that I wasn't worried nor afraid of him, and to this day, I am still not. He'll never realize how many times I've spared his life; even convincing myself not to retaliate. However, he should thank his lucky stars and my Christian beliefs for ordering my steps; especially after he came to me again and threatened another person that I love.

I was out getting some exercise when a car approached me. I ignored it and continued to walk because many cars had passed with people waving and saying hello to me as they passed. I didn't pay the car any mind, but when it slowed down, I looked at it and tried to figure out who it belonged to. I didn't recognize it, so when it came to a stop, I also stopped and looked in at the driver. When the driver leaned out, it was Hicks's cousin. I guess my uncle's threat must have fallen on his deaf ears because he immediately threatened me and said, "I've been seeing your daughter riding her bike around here, and one of these days when I see her I'm going to get her, and you won't even be able to recognize her when you see her again." When he said this, something went all over me, and I said, "If you go anywhere near my daughter, I'll kill you nigga!" When I said this, he quickly sped off. I should have immediately gone to the police about the threat and the incident, but as I walked home; I devised an actual plan to kill him instead. I was so angry that I didn't even care anymore about the consequences. He had to be stopped because he'd already gotten away with so much for so long. Plus, I rationalized if he would even be missed if he were gone.

Apparently, I was no killer, so that's why Hicks's cousin is still alive today. Instead of following through on my plan of revenge after he threatened my daughter's life, I decided to move her away instead. We moved to Portland, Oregon; a safe environment where she was free to ride her bike and be a kid. In Oregon, she blossomed in to a smart, brave, and strong woman; like the one I wished I could have been at her age. She has many of her dad's characteristics, but she is very protective like me, and will go through great lengths to make sure no one is wronged while in her presence. However, my daughter has her own personality too, and that is as a tough motivator. If you want to anger her; just show her that you're trying to give up or lack faith in yourself. She hates the word "I can't." I can truly say that she is what has kept me strong and going all these years when I wanted to give up. Yep, that's the gem that Hicks and I created; our Krystal.

Some years later, and with me no longer living in Alabama, Hicks's cousin would try out his micro aggression again, but this time it would be with one of my younger brothers. The incident happened during a visit to our dad's house. He and our mom finally split, and after their separation, he started a new relationship with Hicks's cousin's mom. Although she created a monster, she was a sweet lady, and my siblings really liked her. I liked her too, and I had already gotten to know her and her children while being Hicks's wife. In fact, she reminded me of his mom because they too had similar features, and she was very clean and could cook like her. She really cared for our dad, and he seemed happy, so this made us like her even more. While discussing her with my dad one day, I even found out that the two were once childhood sweethearts, so they had history. With my dad and his new old sweetheart in a relationship; our families would now have to mesh. It also meant that my family would now have to be in the presence of Hicks's cousin, and it wasn't long before he and my brother's personalities clashed.

The night of the incident, my brother dropped by to see our dad. When he entered the house, he saw that our dad was entertaining several of his friends, and he said Hicks's cousin was there visiting his mom. Shortly after he arrived, Hicks's cousin started antagonizing our dad's guests; using foul and disrespectful language while talking to them. My brother said he could tell he'd had too much to drink, so he asked him to settle down and show respect for our dad's friends and his house. After he told the cousin this, he leaped from his seat in to my brother's face and said, "I ain't never liked you because you think you're something, but I'll have you screaming just like I had your brother-in-law!" My brother said his statement not only shocked him, but it made him go in to a rage. He said he even believe that he blacked out until he heard the screams from his dad's friends. When he came to himself, he saw the cousin underneath him beaten and bloody. I later called my dad from Oregon and asked about the incident. He said that he thought that my brother was going to kill him, and so did his mother. He also said that if he hadn't had help removing my brother, he probably would've.

I understood my brother's fury, and I knew it was pay back for the pain he was caused. He was only twelve years old when Hicks died, and he looked up to him and loved him. If he even heard Hicks's car in the distance, he'd race out the house and wait for him to arrive. All my siblings loved him and took it hard when he died, but this little brother took it the hardest, and I remember his cries throughout that night. Now, there stood the man responsible for his beloved brother in-law's death; confessing and gloating before him, so he lost it, and he had every right to. After the incident, Hicks's cousin took my brother to court, and sued him for his injuries. However, when my brother told the judge what he'd said to him; the case was thrown out, and Hicks's cousin was then charged with disturbing the peace. To this day, he is still roaming the area being a nuisance. I constantly hear stories about him getting beat up, thrown through car windows, and shot at. Last time I saw him, he looked like a corpse that hadn't died yet. However, what upset me most is knowing that the man who help take my husband's life, now has kids and grandkids. I'm angry because he stole this possibility from Hicks, my daughter, and my grandchildren, and it's not fair. I know that God is the ultimate equalizer, and whenever He decides to handle things, it will be handled just like he did with the others; it involved a lot of long suffering too. No, the ones involved in Hicks's death, haven't dropped quickly like flies, but the process has shown me that vengeance is indeed God's. He would later allow me to be present to hear about another one, and this death and the timing of it; would not only shock me, but it would prove that God is also long suffering.

After living in Oregon for five years with my daughter, we caught a flight and came home to Alabama for a visit. I think she was seventeen during that time. When we landed, my brother picked us up from the airport, and transported us to our mother's house. Almost all my siblings, nieces, and nephews were there when we arrived, and it felt good being home. We ate good food and stayed up all night catching up. It wasn't until daybreak that we all finally decided to go to bed. However, I still got up early and started preparing breakfast for everyone while they slept. The kitchen felt lonely, so I decided to turn on the radio to fill in the quiet emptiness. When the music came on, it was like a dream. It filled the room with wonderful R&B tunes that I had now become unaccustomed to; since Oregon at the time, had no R&B stations. The music was literally melting away my jet lag and tiredness from being in another time zone, and it seemed to propel me through my culinary tasks.

I'd finally finished cooking, and I was taking the biscuits from the oven when the DJ interrupted with breaking news. He announced that a woman had been found dead in her front yard, and then he explained to the listeners who she was. When he said her name, I almost dropped the pan that I was holding. It was the preacher's third wife; the one who had called me that night asking me to come to her house because she had something to tell me, the one that was the aunt of the brown eyed girl that had been murdered, and the one that had the big yard fire after her husband's death. My mind was swirling, and I literally had to stop it so I could finish hearing the DJ's commentary. After he told his listeners the woman's name, he went on to tell them how they may have remembered her. He relayed that she was the third wife to the Reverend that was murdered at the funeral of her sixteen-year-old niece. Then the DJ told his listeners how she died. He said that she was found on her lawn stabbed to death. He didn't give any further details about her murder but said there were no suspects. He then stated that he'd give further information once it developed. I stood there in shock and felt light headed from the news. I wondered who could have taken her life after all those years, and I wondered what she'd done to the individual that killed her. Almost fourteen years after Hicks's death, and five years of being in Oregon, I couldn't believe how that news waited for me to come back home to Alabama, so I could hear it.

Over the years, I continue to get information about different deaths of people who were my suspects in Hicks's demise, and I continue to get bits and pieces about Hicks and his uncle also. One day, I went to buy a car, and ended up meeting a salesman that knew my family. He then inquired if I were married, and I told him about my current husband, and then relayed who my previous husband was. When I said Hicks's name, he immediately stopped me then told me he'd met him. He then said, "I met him and his uncle." I was in shock and disbelief after I heard his statement. He went on to say that he was twenty years old at the time, and he was working for a local auto finance company when the two came in and purchased a red Firebird. He said that he was in training, so he was even present during the signing of the auto contract. He told me that Hicks's uncle put a small amount down, and then took out an insurance policy on the car. He remembered that the policy signed, had a clause that stated that the contract and car would be satisfied and paid in full upon Hicks's death. He then said, "They never made one payment on that car, and I know because I was the one that had to make the collection calls." After weeks of non-payment, his boss even sent him to Hicks's uncle's house and threatened him with repossession. He then laughed and said, "You know what, I don't think we ever got payment on that car, and I don't ever remember seeing it again, so what happened to it?" I stood staring at him in disbelief then said, "Well, Hicks was found dead in it, and I never even got to see the car's condition, so like you, I never saw it again." The salesman wagged his head, and said how it was a shame that happened, and we moved on to my purchase. However, I remembered asking Hicks's mom about the car, and she told me that it was sold, but would never tell me who sold it, nor to whom it was sold. That secret also went to the grave.

Hicks's death taught me that you can never be too careful about who you allow to lurk in your inner circle, and this includes family. I have endured many sleepless nights thinking about him. When sleep did find me, he'd come to me in dreams and would try to tell me what happened, but each time I'd wake up, or someone would wake me up before he could. Afterwards, I'd spend the whole day feeling puzzled and upset. In my last most recent one, he came to me and asked that I not forget him, nor let our daughter forget. This dream was so vivid, and I felt his presence even after I woke up. I believe that his spirit's not only seeking rest, but it is also seeking justice; I hope this book will do just that.

When you die young, you miss out on so much. It saddens me knowing that Hicks not only missed out on his daughter's life, but also on the lives of his three handsome grandsons; especially the one that look exactly like him. It is strange knowing that he is a grandpa, yet he didn't even live long enough to become one. In fact, his oldest grandson is older than his body's current state. We often take trips to my former small community, and when we do, our youngest grandchild always ask to visit his grave. The last time we were there, I listened as my grandson talked to him. He said, "Grandpa, I'm sorry that you can't be here with us and hope you are sleeping well, but I wish that I could have gotten to see you and spend time with you before you died." His words pricked my heart, and I stood there wiping my tears while trying to hide them. I love spending time with my boys, and I know Hicks would have too because I saw how he was with my younger brothers. He would have had his grandsons driving and working on cars before they were old enough to drive too.

As for our daughter, she is still deeply hurt by her dad's unexplained death and absence from her life. Although she has coped with the loss, it was difficult for her once we left Alabama, and she no longer had my dad and uncles around to fill in the fatherly gaps. Her senior year in high school was especially difficult. She was selected as Debutant for her school and had to seek out a dad for the "Father Daughter" dance portion of the ceremony. She eventually chose an older member from our church to fill in. Father's Day is also another trying time for her, and I've noticed how sad she becomes when she sees others celebrating with their dads.

One day, I reluctantly asked my daughter if she had any memories of her dad, and she could only recall four small ones. One memory was of him working on his car as she played on a bouncy-horse we'd gotten her. She told me she remembered her dad getting on to her about bouncing too high, and warned her that if she didn't stop, it would flip over. Her next memory was him scolding her for crying loudly in the middle of the night after she awoke to find him gone from our bed. She remembered walking through a house looking for him and was crying because she was afraid. She said once she got to some steps that led to a dark room, she was afraid to go down them, so she stood there calling out to her dad. After her cries, she heard her dad's voice telling her to hush the noise, and then he came to her and picked her up. She said he placed her in a bed with another bed on top of it, and she recalled snuggling up to him as he wrapped his arms around her making her feel safe. I knew it was Hicks's family's house that she remembered because they had an area where all the men slept that lived there. Hicks had a bed in that area too, and he slept on a bottom bunk. Even though Hicks and I had our own bedroom in the house, he would often sneak off there so he could escape our daughter's wild sleeping habits. My daughter's third memory was a fun one, and to my surprise, even at two years old, she'd driven her dad's car. She said he let her sit in his lap and steer the car while he shifted the gears. Her fourth memory was also a fun and happy one, but when she told it to me, I became sad because I knew it was her last. She recalled jumping on a bed near a window that faced Kentucky Fried Chicken, as her dad laughed and told her to jump higher. I recalled her memory too because the three of us would often have weekend getaways, and we would stay at Bob White's Hotel in Alexander, City that was right across from the restaurant. After hearing snippets of her memories, I couldn't help but to thank God for allowing her to keep them; even though she told me that they came with no clear memory of his face.

As for me, Hicks's death left many open wounds that have yet to heal. I still struggle with being happy because a large part of me died with him. Also, I am still in denial that he is gone, and I often find myself longing to see him. What hurts me the most, is that my young husband was murdered, and after all these years, I still don't know exactly how he died. All the murders were covered by several newspapers and magazines; even featured in the 1977 edition of Jet, but it only focused on Hicks's uncle. No-one has ever tried to solve Hicks's death, so I want his case reopened. Currently, all I have are my suspicions, an incomplete death certificate that no one cared enough to complete, and an unclear autopsy report that no one cared enough to conclude. To this day, those documents still read, "Death Unknown," and that is why I am still in limbo and seeking closure after all this time. However, my prayer is that this book will spark a new interest in to Hicks's life and death; while helping to unravel other mysteries behind it. I know that it won't bring him back to us, but it will bring all our family closure, and it would finally unearth all his "Grave Secrets."

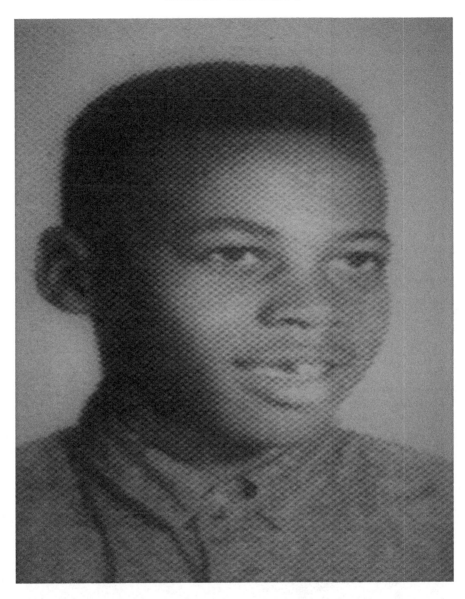

MARY HICKS GUNN

ALABAMA
Center for Health Statistics

STATE OF ALABAMA
CERTIFICATE OF DEATH

No. 5242

Name	James Edward Hicks
Date of Death	February 16, 1976
Race	Black
Sex	M
Age	22
Date of Birth	3-29-53
County of Death	Coosa County
Place of Birth	Cottage Grove, Ala.
State	Alabama
Citizen	U.S.A.
Marital Status	Married
Spouse	Mrs. Mary Dean Hicks
SSN	416-74-2694
Occupation	Mill Worker
Industry	Textiles
Residence	General Delivery
Father	James Edward Hicks
Mother	Ella Maxwell
Informant	Mrs. Mary Dean Hicks, General Delivery, Nixburg, Ala.
Coroner	Jimmy Bailey, Goodwater, Ala.
Cause of Death	autopsy pending
Burial	2-21-76, Pepps & Goodwill, Cottage Grove, Alabama
Funeral Home	Arbour Funeral Home, P.O. Box 713, Alex City, Ala.

This is an official certified copy of the original record filed in the Center of Health Statistics, Alabama Department of Public Health, Montgomery, Alabama. 2915-221-492-0

STATE OF ALABAMA
DEPARTMENT OF TOXICOLOGY
AND
CRIMINAL INVESTIGATION
AUBURN, ALABAMA

May 20, 1976

Re: Case 1(P)-125388 AB
James Edward Hicks, subject

MEMORANDUM: To File

BY : Vann V. Pruitt, Jr., Toxicologist

SUBJECT : Postmortem Examination

Monday, February 16, 1976, at 12:18 PM CST, the body of James Edward Hicks was examined at the Armour Funeral Home, Alexander City, Alabama. This body was examined upon the authority of District Attorney Harold Walden and subsequent to the request of Coosa County Coroner Jimmy Bailey. At the time the body was examined it had not been embalmed and was still clothed. The body was clothed in a red, short sleeve, knit shirt, a pair of denim trousers, a denim jacket, black ankle boots, and black socks. A string of beads was present around the neck. A Coosa County High School class ring dated "1971" was present on the right ring finger. A silver identification bracelet bearing the name "Belinda" was present on the right wrist. A ring with a pale-blue stone was present on the right little finger.

EXTERNAL EXAMINATION:

The body presented for examination externally was determined to be that of a Negro male measuring 5 feet 8-1/2 inches in length, weighing an estimated 120 to 130 pounds, and appearing consistent with the reported approximate 23 years of age. The head hair was black in color. There was a thin mustache on the upper lip and a growth of beard about the chin. The build was described as slender. The irides were brown in color; the pupils were fixed and clear. The upper front teeth were missing and the general repair of those remaining appeared rather poor. There was an old scar in the left shoulder midway between the base of the neck and the tip of the shoulder on the left side which measured 1 inch. The body was cold to touch and rigor was only mild with each of the extremities capable of being flexed with only little difficulty. Livor was markedly observed about the posterior torso. The impression of the various items of clothing, including the beads about the neck, were firmly

CERT
SENT

Page 2 — Postmortem Examination, Case 1(P)-173388 AB, May 20, 1973

marked into the surface of the chest and about the neck and the upper arms. The right lateral upper abdomen appeared markedly greenish in coloration extending upward and across a line correlating to that of the ascending and transverse colon. The following injuries were noted on or about the body:

1. Two very small superficial abrasions were noted about the anterior left lower leg. One measured 2-1/2 inches and the other measured 1-1/2 inches.

2. There was a 3-inch superficial abrasion on the anterior left upper leg.

3. There was a superficial abrasion measuring 1/2 inch across located on the lower anterior right leg, and another similar superficial abrasion about the right lateral knee measuring 1/2 inch in diameter.

4. There was a superficial contusion about the anterior middle upper right leg.

5. There was a superficial abrasion on the right outer upper arm at the shoulder which measured 1/2 inch by 5/8 inch.

6. There was an abrasion across the lower right rib cage 2 inches to the right of the midline which measured 3/4 inch in width and extended 1 inch in length.

7. There were two small abrasions, each measuring 1/2 inch across, located in the lower right rib cage immediately above the previously described abrasion.

8. There was a small laceration on the lower inner lip. A small amount of blood was purging from the left corner of the mouth.

There was no other evidence of injuries noted on or about the body externally.

CRANIAL:

The scalp was incised using a transbregmatic incision. The forward and backward flaps were reflected and the undersurfaces examined. There was no evidence of sub-scalp bruising or bone fragments or fractures noted. Entry into the calvaria disclosed a small subdural hematoma about the left frontal-parietal area. The maximum amount of hemorrhage was estimated as being approximately 50 cc's. Examination of the brain revealed it to be apparently symmetrical, somewhat flattened and markedly softened evidencing early postmortem decomposition changes. There were no apparent ruptures of the blood vessels comprising the circle of Willis. Examination of the basal portion of the brain revealed mild bilateral herniation in the uncal areas with bilateral cerebellar protrusion through the tentorium. Sectioning of the brain failed to disclose evidence of intracranial hemorrhage or lesions.

Page 3 - Postmortem Examination, Case 1(F)-125388 AR, May 20, 1976

THORACIC-ABDOMINAL:

The thoracic and abdominal cavities were opened utilizing a Y-shaped incision. The organs contained within the thoracic and abdominal cavities were examined.

Organs of the Neck: An extension of the Y-shaped incision was made in order to reveal the musculature and organs of the neck. Examination of the major musculature of the neck failed to show evidence of bruising or hemorrhage within the muscle sheaths. There was no evidence of hemorrhage or bruising of the thyroid. The tracheobronchial tree was unobstructed and there was no evidence of fractures of the hyoid bone or the thyroid and cricoid cartilages.

Lungs and Cavities: Both lungs were collapsed within their respective pleural cavities and were subcrepitant and appeared somewhat bright red in color. A small quantity of tannish-colored fluid was contained in each cavity. The organs could be removed without any difficulty of adhesions. Sectioning of the organs revealed evidence of postmortem change with no evidence of significant lesions or any indication of trauma.

Heart: Examination of the heart failed to reveal any apparent occlusion of the coronary vessels. The organ itself was present in its normal location with a minimal distribution of fat over its surface. There was no evidence of gross defects on sectioning the various chambers of the heart. The valves were pliable and without any evidence of anomaly.

Liver: Examination of the liver revealed the margins to be distinct, the surface smooth with some marked staining of bile about the area of the gallbladder with a rather softening feel to the organ in general associated with postmortem change. Sectioning failed to reveal any evidence of lesions.

Gastrointestinal: Examination of the stomach and intestinal tract revealed a very small quantity of dark-appearing fluid in the stomach without any marked evidence of inflammation of the gastric lining. The intestinal tract was not particularly remarkable in its appearance. There was present an accumulation of gas attributable to postmortem change.

Spleen: The spleen was rather small in size, somewhat pulpy. Examination of the organ failed to reveal any evidence of lacerations.

Pancreas: The pancreas was not remarkable. There was no evidence of any hemorrhage or other lesions.

Adrenal Gland: Each adrenal gland was present in its normal suprarenal position and upon sectioning presented the normal appearing yellowish cortex with the grayish-red medulla. There was no evidence of medullary swelling or hemorrhage.

Kidneys: The kidneys were each in their normal location and could be removed from the renal beds without difficulty. Their surfaces stripped without difficulty and were smooth. Sectioning disclosed the usual demarcation

Page 4 - Postmortem Examination, Case 217J-125348 AA, May 20, 1976

between the cortical and the pyramidal areas. There was no evidence of increments within the renal pelves or the ureters.

Genitalia: The penis was uncircumcised and the testes had descended.

Skeletal: Examination of the skeletal system failed to reveal any evidence of apparent fractures.

CONCLUSION:

Examination of the above described body failed to disclose the exact mechanism of death. Although there were some superficial trauma described externally on the body, there was no subsequent injury involving any of the organs examined which would adequately account for the death of this subject. The very minimal quantity of hemorrhage in the brain with only mild evidence of any swelling produced fails to clearly illustrate the mechanism of death as involving trauma to the head. The condition of the organs as a result of postmortem change was such as to preclude histopathological studies. Specimens of the various tissues and body fluids were returned to the laboratory for analyses to detect the presence of drugs and/or poisons.

VWP:cfv/29/A02

Made in the USA
Monee, IL
06 July 2020